شرح رياض الصالحين

باب المبادرة إلى الخيرات

Explanation of Riyaadh Saliheen:
THE CHAPTER ON HASTENING TOWARDS GOOD DEEDS

Author of (Riyaadh Saliheen):
Abu Zakariya Yahya bin Sharaf An-Nawawi (676 AH)

Explanation by: Shaykh Muhammad Bin Saleh al-'Uthaymeen

© Maktabatulirshad Publications, USA

All rights reserved. No part of this publication may be reproduced in any language, stored in any retrieval system or transmitted in any form or by any means, whether electronic, mechanic, photocopying, recording or otherwise, without express permission of the copyright owner.

First Edition: Shawwal 1434 A.H. / August 2013 C.E.

Cover Design: Strictly Sunnah Designs
E-mail: info@strictlysunnahdesigns.com

Translation by Aboo Yusuf 'Abdullaah Ibrahim Omran Al-Misri

Revision of Translation by: Rasheed Ibn Estes Barbee

Typesetting and Editing: Aboo Sulaymaan Muhammad 'Abdul-Azim bin Joshua Baker

Subject: Hadeeth

Website: www.maktabatulirshad.com
E-mail: info@maktabatulirshad.com

فِهْرِس

Table Of Contents

BIOGRAPHY OF THE EXPLAINER 4
INTRODUCTION 11
   The Explanation 11
HADITH NUMBER 87..33
   The Explanation 34
HADITH NUMBER 88..42
   The Explanation 43
HADITH NUMBER 89..51
   The Explanation 51
HADITH NUMBER 90..56
   The Explanation 56
HADITH NUMBER 91..61
   The Explanation 62
HADITH NUMBER 92..67
   The Explanation 67
HADITH NUMBER 93..77
   The Explanation 78
HADITH NUMBER 94..88
   The Explanation 90

BIOGRAPHY OF THE EXPLAINER
Al-Allaamah Muhammad Bin Saleh Al-'Uthaymeen (1347-1421AH)

His lineage and birth: He is the noble scholar, verifier, Faqeeh, scholar of Tafsir, god-fearing, ascetic, Muhammad Bin Saleh Bin Muhammad bin Sulaymaan bin 'Abd-Rahman Ali 'Uthaymeen from *Al-Wahbah* of Bani Tameem. He was born on the 27th night of the blessed month Ramadan in the year 1347AH in 'Unayzah –one of the cities of Al-Qaseem- in the kingdom of Saudia Arabia.

His scholastic upbringing: his father, may Allâh have mercy upon him, enrolled him to study the Noble Quran with his maternal grandfather, the teacher 'Abdur-Rahman Bin Sulaymaan Ad-Daamigh', may Allâh have mercy upon him. Then he studied writing, some arithmetic, and Arabic literature at *"Al-Ustaadh 'Abdul-Azeez Bin Saleh Ad-Daamigh's school"*; and that was before he enrolled in *"Al-Mu'allim 'Ali Bin 'Abdillah Ash-Shahaytan's School"* where he memorized the Noble Quran with him, and he had not reached fourteen years of age yet.

Under the direction of his father, may Allâh have mercy upon him, he embarked upon seeking religious knowledge; and the noble Shaykh Al-'Allamah 'Abdur Rahman Bin Nasir As-Sa'dee, may Allâh have mercy upon him, use to teach religious sciences and Arabic at *"Jaame' Kabeer"* (i.e. Grand masjid where Jumu'ah his held) in 'Unayzah. He arranged two of his senior students to teach the beginning students. Therefore, the Shaykh (i.e. Al-'Uthaymeen) would join Shaykh Muhammad Bin 'Abdul-'Azeez Al-Mutawwa's circle of knowledge, may Allâh have mercy upon him, until he attained from knowledge of *Tawheed, Fiqh,* and *Nahw* (i.e. Arabic grammar related to the ending of words) what he attained.

Then he sat in the circles of knowledge of his Shaykh 'Abdur Rahman Bin Nasir As-Sa'dee, may Allâh have mercy upon him. So he studied with him Tafsir, Hadith, Seerah of the Prophet, At-Tawheed, Al-Fiqh, Al-'Usool, Al-Faraa'id, An-Nahw, and memorization concise texts on these sciences.

BIOGRAPHY OF THE EXPLAINER

The noble Shaykh Al-'Allamah 'Abdur Rahman Bin Nasir As-Sa'dee, May Allâh have mercy upon him, was considered to be his first Shaykh. Since he acquired knowledge, experience, and methods (of learning) from him more so than anyone else; and he was impressed by his methodology, his principles, his way of teaching, and his adherence to proofs and evidences.

When Shaykh 'Abdur-Rahman Bin 'Ali Bin 'Awdaan, may Allâh have mercy upon him, was a judge in 'Unayzah he (i.e. Shaykh Al-'Uthaymeen) would study the science of Al-Faraa'id with him, just like he would study An-Nahw and Al-Balaghah with Shaykh 'Abdur-Razzaaq 'Afeefee, may Allâh have mercy upon him, during his presence as a teacher in that city.

When the academic institution opened in Riyadh, some of his brothers urged him to enroll. So he sought his Shaykh's, 'Abdur Rahman Bin Nasir As-Sa'dee, may Allâh have mercy upon him, permission. So he gave him permission, and he enrolled in the institution from 1372AH to 1373AH.

EXPLANATION OF RIYAADH SALIHEEN: THE CHAPTER ON HASTENING TO GOOD DEEDS

Indeed he took advantage of the scholars who use to teach there at that time, through the two years that he entered in the academic institution in Riyadh. Among them was Al-'Allamah, scholar in Tafsir Shaykh Muhammad Al-Ameen As-Shanqitee, Shaykh Al-Faqeeh 'Abdul-'Azeez Bin Nasir Bin Rasheed, and Shaykh, the scholar in hadith, 'Abdur-Rahman Al-Ifreekee...may Allâh have mercy upon them.

During that time, he would stick with His eminence Shaykh Al-'Allamah 'Abdul-'Azeez Bin 'Abdillah Bin Baaz, may Allâh have mercy upon him, and he studied with him Saheeh Bukhari and some treatises of Shaykhul-Islam Ibn Taymiyah in the masjid. He benefited by him in the science of hadith, analyzing the views of the scholars of fiqh and the relationship between them. He considered Shaykh 'Abdul-'Azeez Bin Baaz, may Allâh have mercy upon him, to be his second Shaykh in obtaining knowledge and being influenced by him.

Then he returned to 'Unayzah in 1374AH, and he commenced studying under his Shaykh Al-'Allamah 'Abdur-Rahman Bin Nasir As-Sa'dee and he followed up his studies in the faculty of Sharee'ah, which had become a subsidiary of

BIOGRAPHY OF THE EXPLAINER

Imam Muhammad Bin Saud Islamic University until he obtained a high-ranking degree.

His teaching: his Shaykh saw in him nobleness and quickness in the acquisition of knowledge, so he encouraged him to teach while he was still a student in his circles of knowledge. So he began teaching in 1370 at the "*Jaamee Kabeer*" in 'Unayzah.

When he graduated from the institute in Riyadh, he was appointed as a teacher at the institution in 'Unayzah in 1374AH.

In 1376AH, his Shaykh Al-'Allamah 'Abdur-Rahman Bin Nasir as-Sa'dee, may Allâh have mercy upon him, died. Therefore, he (i.e. Al-'Uthaymeen) was appointed the imamate of "Jaamee Kabeer" in 'Unayzah and also he was appointed the imamate of two 'Eid there, and he was appointed to teach in the library of 'Unayzah Al-Wataniyah next to Jaamee Kabeer, which his Shaykh, founded in 1359AH.

When the number of students increased, and the library could not suffice them, the noble Shaykh began teaching in the Masjid Al-Jaamee. The students gathered there, and they would flock together from Kingdom of Saudia Arabia

EXPLANATION OF RIYAADH SALIHEEN: THE CHAPTER ON HASTENING TO GOOD DEEDS

and outside of the Kingdom until they reached in the hundreds for some of the classes. These people studied seriously, and they did not just simply listened to the classes. He (i.e. 'Uthaymeen) remained upon that as an Imam, a Khateeb, and a teacher until his passing, may Allâh have mercy upon him.

The Shaykh remained a teacher in the institution from 1374AH to 1398AH, and when he transferred to teaching in the faculty of *Sharee'ah* and *Usool-Deen* in Al-Qaseem branch to Muhammad Bin Saud Islamic University and remained as a teacher there until his passing away, May Allâh the most high have mercy upon him.

He use to lecture in *Masjid Haram* and *Masjid An-Nabawi* during the seasons of Hajj, Ramadan, and the summer vacations from 1402AH until his passing away, may Allâh have mercy upon him.

The Shaykh had a particular teaching practice in his openhandedness and integrity. He would raise questions to his students, receive their questions, and hold classes and lectures with a lofty concern, a composed mind and delighted at

BIOGRAPHY OF THE EXPLAINER

his propagating religious knowledge and his closeness to the people.

His passing away: He passed away, may Allaah have mercy upon him, in the city of Jeddah shortly before Maghrib on Wednesday the 15th of the month of Shawwal 1421AH. He was prayed over in *Masjid Haram* after 'Asr on Thursday. Then he was followed by thousands who had prayed over him, and he was buried in *Mecca Al-Mukaramah*. [1]

---

[1] The source of this is biography was from the Shaykh's website (www.ibnothaimeen.com)

EXPLANATION OF RIYAADH SALIHEEN: THE CHAPTER ON HASTENING TO GOOD DEEDS

INTRODUCTION

The author (Imam Nawawi) 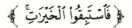 said,

Urging whoever pursues good deeds to be steadfast, without hesitation. Allaah says,

﴿ فَٱسْتَبِقُوا۟ ٱلْخَيْرَٰتِ ﴾

"So hasten towards all that is good."[2]

And Allaah says,

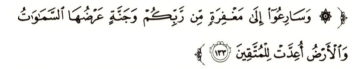

"And march forth in the way (which leads to) forgiveness from your Lord, and for Paradise as wide as are the heavens and the earth, prepared for Al-Muttaqûn (the pious)." [3]

The Explanation

The author - rahimahullah- stated,

"Hastening for good deeds and urging whoever pursues good deeds to be determined sustaining no hesitation."

[2] al-Baqarah[2: 148]
[3] Al-Imran [3:133]

INTRODUCTION

This title implies two points:

Firstly: Hastening and taking the initiative to do good deeds.

Secondly: If the person is determined to do something good, he/she should proceed without hesitation.

The first point is initiative which opposes laziness and slackness. The person who is lazy and slack has missed plenty of good deeds. The prophet Muhammad ﷺ ('alayhi salātu wa salaam) said,

الْمُؤْمِنُ الْقَوِيُّ خَيْرٌ وَ أَحَبُّ إِلَى اللهِ مِنَ الْمُؤْمِنِ الضَّعِيفِ، وَ فِي كُلِّ خَيْرٍ، احْرِصْ عَلَى مَا يَنْفَعُكَ وَاسْتَعِنْ بِاللهِ وَ لَا تَعْجَزْ

"The strong believer is better and more beloved to Allaah than the weak believer, although both are good. Strive to do that which will benefit you and seek the help of Allaah, and do not feel helpless."[4]

The individual should hasten to do good deeds as soon as he is told about them such as Salah, Sadaqah (charity), Sawm (fasting), Hajj (pilgrimage), obedience to the parents, retaining ties of kinship and so on. The individual should

---

[4] Recorded by Muslim: (2664).

hasten to perform these good deeds because he/she does not know if they will be (physically) able to do these deeds after missing it due to death, sickness, or something else. The Messenger of Allaah ﷺ ('alayhi salātu wa salaam) said,

إِذَا أَرَادَ أَحَدُكُمُ الْحَجَّ فَلْيَتَعَجَّلْ ، فَإِنَّهُ قَدْ يَمْرَضُ الْمَرِيضُ ، وَ تَضِلُّ الرَّاحِلَةُ ، وَ تَعْرِضُ الْحَاجَةُ

"**Whoever intends to perform Hajj, let him hasten to do so, for he may fall sick, lose his mount, or be faced with some need.**"[5]

Something may appear (suddenly) and prevent the individual from proceeding to do good deed. Hence, one should hasten to do good deeds and shun laziness. The author then quoted,

﴿ فَٱسْتَبِقُوا۟ ٱلْخَيْرَٰتِ ﴾

"**hasten towards all that is good.**"

This word '**hasten**' is more eloquent than '**race**' because it prompts the person to gain the lead

---

5 - Recorded by Ibn Majah: (2883), Ahmad: (1/214). It has other versions recorded by Abu Dawud: (1732), Ahmad: (1/225), al-Hakim: (1/448), and others. It's graded as Hasan by al-Albani: Sahih al-Jami': (6004).

INTRODUCTION

in scoring good deeds. Similarly, hastening to catch the first row in Salah. The Messenger of Allaah ﷺ (sallallahu 'alayhi wa sallam) said,

خَيْرُ صُفُوفِ الرِّجَالِ أَوَّلُهَا، وَ شَرُّهَا آخِرُهَا، وَ خَيْرُ صُفُوفِ النِّسَاءِ آخِرُهَا، وَ شَرُّهَا أَوَّلُهَا.

"The best rows for men are the first rows, and the worst ones the last ones, and the best rows for women are the last ones and the worst ones for them are the first ones."[6]

The prophet ﷺ (salallahu 'alayhi wa sallam) saw some people in the rear of the Masjid who haven't raced nor approached to the front (rows); he therefore said,

لَا يَزَالُ قَوْمٌ يَتَأَخَّرُونَ حَتَّى يُؤَخِّرَهُمُ اللهُ عَزَّ وَ جَلَّ.

"People will continue to keep back till Allaah will put them at the back."[7]

So seize this opportunity and hasten to do good deeds. Allaah says,

---

[6] Recorded by Muslim: Book of prayer: Chapter: Straightening the Rows: (440).
[7] Recorded by Muslim: Book of prayer: Chapter: Straightening the Rows: (438).

EXPLANATION OF RIYAADH SALIHEEN: THE CHAPTER ON HASTENING TO GOOD DEEDS

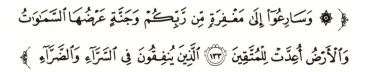

"And march forth in the way (which leads to) forgiveness from your Lord, and for Paradise as wide as are the heavens and the earth, prepared for Al-Muttaqûn (the pious). Those who spend [in Allaah's Cause] in prosperity and in adversity ...."[8]

Allaah said:

'March forth in the way that leads to forgiveness and paradise.'

As for marching forth to seek forgiveness: the person should pursue means of forgiveness like saying:

Astaghfirullah! (I ask Allaah's forgiveness) or O Allaah! Forgive me and so on. Besides, ablution, the five (daily) prayers, back-to-back Jumu'ah, and back-to-back (fasting) Ramadhaan. If the person perfected his/her ablution and then said: I bear witness that there is no God (worthy of worship) but You, and I bear witness that Muhammad is Your servant and messenger. (Allahumma ij'alni minat-tawwabina waj'alni

---

[8] Al-Imran [3:133-134]

INTRODUCTION

minAl-mutatahhirina) "O Allaah! Include me among those who repent and those who keep themselves pure, the eight gates of paradise will be open for him/her and they have free choice to enter from whichever gate they desire[9]. I addition, if the person made ablution, his/her sins would come out of the parts of the body exposed to the water to the last drop of water.[10] **These are causes of forgiveness.**

Furthermore, the five daily prayers, back-to-back Jumu'ahs, back-to-back (fasting) Ramadhaan purge sins committed between them as long as major sins are not committed.[11]

The second matter:

﴿ وَجَنَّةٍ عَرْضُهَا ٱلسَّمَوَٰتُ وَٱلۡأَرۡضُ ﴾

"Paradise as wide as are the heavens and the earth."

This is acquired through implementing our assigned obligations. **It means:** to march forth in the way (that leads) to paradise through

---

[9] Recorded by al-Tirmidhi in its full narration in chapter of purification: (55). It's also recorded by Muslim. Book of Purification: chapter of: "admirable Dhikr to be said after ablution" without the portion of "O Allaah! Include me among those who repent and those who keep themselves pure." (234)

[10] It's narrated from the authority of Abu Hurairah (Marfu'). Recorded by Muslim. Book of purification: chapter of Purging of Sins with Ablution Water: (244).

[11] Narrated by Abu Hurairah, and recorded by Muslim. Book of purification: chapter of: five daily prayers and back-to-back Jumu'ahs: (233).

EXPLANATION OF RIYAADH SALIHEEN: THE CHAPTER ON HASTENING TO GOOD DEEDS

committing oneself to good deeds only, which is the key for entering paradise. Allaah has informed us that the paradise is as wide as heavens and earth, which implies its spaciousness and wideness and that no one gives it its true estimate except for Allaah. So, hasten and seize all forms of good deeds that lead you to paradise.

Allaah says,

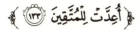

"prepared for Al-Muttaqûn (the pious)."

Allaah is the one who prepared it for them as mentioned in the Hadith Qudsi,

أَعْدَدْتُ لِعِبَادِي الصَّالِحِينَ مَا لَا عَيْنٌ رَأَتْ، وَ لَا أُذُنٌ سَمِعَتْ، وَ لَا خَطَرَ عَلَى قَلْبِ بَشَرٍ.

"Allaah said, 'I have prepared for My pious worshipers such things as no eye has ever seen, no ear has ever heard of, and nobody has ever thought of.'"[12]

But who are the pious? Allaah says,

---

[12] Recorded by Al-Bukhari. Book of the beginning of creation. Chapter of the hadiths describing the virtue of paradise: (3244), and Muslim. Book of paradise: chapter of the description of paradise: (2824).

INTRODUCTION

﴿ ٱلَّذِينَ يُنفِقُونَ فِى ٱلسَّرَّآءِ وَٱلضَّرَّآءِ وَٱلْكَـٰظِمِينَ ٱلْغَيْظَ وَٱلْعَافِينَ عَنِ ٱلنَّاسِ ۗ وَٱللَّهُ يُحِبُّ ٱلْمُحْسِنِينَ ۞ وَٱلَّذِينَ إِذَا فَعَلُوا۟ فَـٰحِشَةً أَوْ ظَلَمُوٓا۟ أَنفُسَهُمْ ذَكَرُوا۟ ٱللَّهَ فَٱسْتَغْفَرُوا۟ لِذُنُوبِهِمْ وَمَن يَغْفِرُ ٱلذُّنُوبَ إِلَّا ٱللَّهُ وَلَمْ يُصِرُّوا۟ عَلَىٰ مَا فَعَلُوا۟ وَهُمْ يَعْلَمُونَ ۞ أُو۟لَـٰٓئِكَ جَزَآؤُهُم مَّغْفِرَةٌ مِّن رَّبِّهِمْ وَجَنَّـٰتٌ تَجْرِى مِن تَحْتِهَا ٱلْأَنْهَـٰرُ خَـٰلِدِينَ فِيهَا ۚ وَنِعْمَ أَجْرُ ٱلْعَـٰمِلِينَ ۞ ﴾

"Those who spend [in Allaah's Cause] in prosperity and in adversity, who repress anger, and who pardon men; verily, Allaah loves Al-Muhsinûn (the good - doers). (134) And those who, when they have committed Fâhishah (illegal sexual intercourse) or wronged themselves with evil, remember Allaah and ask forgiveness for their sins; - and none can forgive sins but Allaah - And do not persist in what (wrong) they have done, while they know. (135) For such, the reward is Forgiveness from their Lord, and Gardens with rivers flowing underneath (Paradise), wherein they shall abide forever. How excellent is this reward for the doers (who do righteous deeds according to Allaah's Orders)." [13]

---

[13] Al Imran [3:134-136]

These are the pious...

$$\{ \text{ٱلَّذِينَ يُنفِقُونَ فِى ٱلسَّرَّآءِ وَٱلضَّرَّآءِ} \}$$

"...who spend [in Allaah's Cause] in prosperity and in adversity."

They spend their wealth in prosperity (i.e. plenty of money and in conditions of happiness), and in adversity (i.e. distress and suffer). However, Allaah has not mentioned the amount they spend but it's mentioned in other verses,

$$\{ \text{وَيَسْـَٔلُونَكَ مَاذَا يُنفِقُونَ قُلِ ٱلْعَفْوَ} \}$$

"And they ask you what they ought to spend. Say: "al-'Afu." [14]

Al-'Afu means: The excess which remains after your needs have been taken care of.

And He also says,

$$\{ \text{وَٱلَّذِينَ إِذَآ أَنفَقُواْ لَمْ يُسْرِفُواْ وَلَمْ يَقْتُرُواْ وَكَانَ بَيْنَ ذَٰلِكَ قَوَامًا} \}$$

"And those, who, when they spend, are neither extravagant nor niggardly, but hold a medium (way) between those (extremes)." [15]

---

[14] Al-Baqarah [2:219]
[15] Al-Furqan [25:67]

INTRODUCTION

$$\text{﴿ وَٱلْكَاظِمِينَ ٱلْغَيْظَ ﴾}$$

"Those who repress anger"

Meaning: when they get so angry, they suppress this anger and don't give it up although the act of suppressing is very hard to execute as the prophet ﷺ (sallallahu 'alayhi wa sallam) said,

$$\text{لَيْسَ الشَّدِيدُ بِالصُّرَعَةِ، وَ لَكِنَّ الشَّدِيدَ الَّذِي يَمْلِكُ نَفْسَهُ عِنْدَ الْغَضَبِ.}$$

"The strong man is not the good wrestler; but the strong man is he who controls himself when he is angry."[16]

The strong person is not the wrestler who defeats people in wrestling, but rather is who suppresses his/her anger because anger creates losing temper, inflation of one's veins, the eyes turn red, and desire for revenge. However, if he/she suppresses this anger and cools off, this will lead to paradise. Know that anger is a firebrand thrown by Satan in the heart of the

---

[16] Recorded by al-Bukhari. Book of Adab: chapter of being cautious from being angry: (6114), and Muslim: The Book of Virtue, Enjoining Good Manners, and Joining of the Ties of Kinship: chapter 'the virtue of who controls his/her anger: (2609).

EXPLANATION OF RIYAADH SALIHEEN: THE CHAPTER ON HASTENING TO GOOD DEEDS

human being when he/she is afflicted with something that shaken him/her up.

The prophet ﷺ (sallallahu 'alayhi wa sallam) has informed us how to smother this firebrand; to seek refuge in Allaah from the outcast Satan when the person gets angry and feels that anger will defeat him/her[17], to sit down if he/she is standing and to lie down if he/she is sitting[18].

Moreover, one should perform ablution[19] by purifying the four organs; the face, the hands,

---

[17] Sulaymaan bin Sarad narrated, **Two men abused each other in front of the Prophet ﷺ (salallahu 'alayhi wa salam) while we were sitting with him. One of the two abused his companion furiously and his face became red. The Prophet ﷺ (salallahu 'alayhi wa salam) said, "I know a word (sentence) the saying of which will cause him to relax if this man says it. Only if he said, "I seek refuge with Allaah from Satan, the outcast."** Recorded by al-Bukhari. Book of Adab: chapter: To be cautious from being angry: (6115) and Muslim. Book of al-Birr wa sillah: chapter 'the virtue of who controls his/her anger. (2610).

[18] Abû Dharr- radiallahu 'anhu- narrated: **The Messenger of Allaah ﷺ (salallahu 'alayhi wa sallam) said to us: "When one of you becomes angry while standing, he should sit down If the anger leaves him, well and good; otherwise he should lie down."** Recorded by Abu Dawud. Book of Adab: chapter: Dhikr to be said during anger (4782). It's graded as Munqati' (i.e. cut off hadith, that which its Isnād is not connected due to a missing link.) but it has graded Mawsool by Ahmad in al-Musnad: (5/152).

[19] AbuWa'il al-Qass said: We entered upon Urwah ibn Muhammad ibn as-Sa'di. A man spoke to him and made him angry. So he stood and performed ablution; he then returned after performing ablution, and said: My father told me on the authority of my grandfather Atiyyah who reported the Messenger of Allaah ﷺ (salallahu 'alayhi wa sallam) as saying: **"Anger**

INTRODUCTION

the head, and the feet as this act suppresses anger. If you ever felt angry, implement this prophetic advice in order for the anger to fade away; otherwise it will cause (unnecessary problems) like separation between married couples. There are a great number of people who express: I was angry with my wife and divorced her three times. The person also may get angry and severely beats his/her children, breaks his/her containers, tears his/her clothes, and so on. Thus, Allaah says,

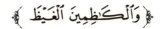

"Those who suppresses anger"

Allaah praised them because they control themselves when anger strikes.

﴿ وَٱلْعَافِينَ عَنِ ٱلنَّاسِ ﴾

"And who pardon men"

Means: they forgive whoever harms them since whoever forgives and sought compromise, his/her reward is with Allaah. The concept of forgiveness is generalized in this verse, but it's detailed in Allaah's saying,

---

comes from the devil, the devil was created of fire, and fire is extinguished only with water; so when one of you becomes angry, he should perform ablution." Recorded by Abu Dawud. Book of AL-Adab: chapter of: what should be said at times of anger: (4784) and Ahmad in al-Musnad: (4/226).

EXPLANATION OF RIYAADH SALIHEEN: THE CHAPTER ON HASTENING TO GOOD DEEDS

﴿ فَمَنْ عَفَا وَأَصْلَحَ ﴾

"If a person forgives and makes reconciliation."[20]

Forgiveness is considered good only if it's accompanied with reconciliation. (For instance) if someone known for harming and transgressing were to harm you, it's better not to forgive him but to claim your right otherwise his transgression will increase. However, if a person is not known for harm nor transgression were to harm you (rarely), it's better to forgive him.

For example, the increasing car accidents. Some people hasten and forgive the guilty person who made the accidents; this is not the right choice, but rather one should consider the following: If this driver is carless and impetuous who does not care about people nor the system, then don't have mercy on him rather claim your full right. By contrast, if this person is known for carefulness, fearing Allaah, discipline, and observant of the system although he committed this accident inadvertently, forgiveness is more appropriate in this situation due to Allaah's saying,

---

[20] Al-Shura [41:40]

INTRODUCTION

> "If a person forgives and makes reconciliation, his/her reward is with Allaah."

So it's a must to consider reconciliation along with forgiveness.

> "Allaah loves Al-Muhsinûn (the good - doers)."

The ultimate purpose of any servant is to be loved by Allaah since every believing person pursues Allaah's love; Allaah says,

> "Say (O Muhammad (sallahu 'alayhi wa sallam) to mankind): "If you (really) love Allaah then follow me (i.e. accept Islâmic Monotheism, follow the Qur'ân and the Sunnah) Allaah will love you." [21]

Allaah has not said: follow me and you be truthful; rather Allaah said: Allaah will love you because the most important of all is that Allaah loves you. I beseech Allaah to make me and you from whom He loves.

The intended individuals by **Al-Muhsinûn** in Allaah's saying,

---

[21] Al-Imran [3:31]

EXPLANATION OF RIYAADH SALIHEEN: THE CHAPTER ON HASTENING TO GOOD DEEDS

﴿ وَٱللَّهُ يُحِبُّ ٱلْمُحْسِنِينَ ﴾

"Allaah loves Al-Muhsinûn." are those who are righteous in worshipping Allaah and act gently with Allaah's servants.

The rank of those who are righteous in worshipping Allaah is mentioned in Jibriel's question to the prophet ﷺ ('alayhi salātu wa sallam) about Ihsân, and the answer was,

أَنْ تَعْبُدَ اللهَ كَأَنَّكَ تَرَاهُ، فَإِنْ لَمْ تَكُنْ تَرَاهُ فَإِنَّهُ يَرَاكَ

"To worship Allaah as if you see Him, and since you don't see Him, know for sure that He sees you."[22]

It means that the person should worship Allaah with a mindful heart as if you see your Lord and want to reach to Him; if you couldn't, know for certain that Allaah sees you. Thus, worship Him out of fear and awe. This latter rank is less in virtue than the first one. The first rank is to worship Allaah out of loving, yearning, and

---

[22] Recorded by al-Bukhari Book of Emaan Chapter of: Gabriel's questions to the prophet ﷺ (salallahu 'alayhi wa sallam) about Emaan: (50), and Muslim. Book of Emaan. Chapter of: what is Emaan: (9) from the authority of Abu Hurairah. It's also narrated from the authority of Umar ibn al-Khattab in Sahih Muslim. Book of Emaan: chapter of: clarification of Emaan, Islam, and Ihsân: (8).

INTRODUCTION

seeking Him; whereas the second is to worship Him out of fear and owe to Him.

As for acting gently with Allaah's servants: is to treat them in the best manner; in speech, actions, generosity, refraining from inflicting harm, and so on. Allaah says,

﴿ وَإِذَا حُيِّيتُم بِتَحِيَّةٍ فَحَيُّوا بِأَحْسَنَ مِنْهَا أَوْ رُدُّوهَا ﴾

"When you are greeted with a greeting, greet in return with what is better than it, or (at least) return it equally." [23]

It means: if you couldn't return the greeting in a better form, you should, at least, greet back. Some scholars maintained thereby, "if a Muslim says: **'As-salaamu alaikum wa rahmatullahi'**, one should reply: **'wa 'alaikum salaam wa rahmatullahi'**; this is the least, and if you were to add: **'wa baarakatuhu'** this is better because Allaah says: return the greeting with what's better. Allaah started with the better then followed it with...

"or return (the greeting) equally."

If a person greeted you in a clear voice, you should, in return, respond clearly at least. Many people return greetings from their nose to the

[23] Al-Nisā' [4:86]

EXPLANATION OF RIYAADH SALIHEEN: THE CHAPTER ON HASTENING TO GOOD DEEDS

extent one almost cannot hear them; this is wrong because this opposes the way they were greeted. You greet one of them with clear voice while he responds with his nose; this is not what Allaah has commanded.

Ihsaan also could be with actions like aiding people with money, charity, or gifts which is a kind of Ihsaan. Likewise, to clarify to your brother (or sister) the sin he/she commits if you noticed it because this is considered among the most beneficial Ihsaan to him/her. The prophet ﷺ ('alayhi salātu wa sallam) said,

اِنْصُرْ أَخَاكَ ظَالِمًا أَوْ مَظْلُومًا، قَالُوا: يَا رَسُولَ الله، هَذَا الْمَظْلُومُ فَكَيْفَ نَنْصُرُ الظَّالِمَ؟ قَالَ: ((أَنْ تَمْنَعَهُ مِنَ الظُّلْمِ)).

"Help your brother whether he is an oppressor or an oppressed," they wandered," O Allaah's messenger: (we understand) about the oppressed; how about the oppressor? He (salallahu 'alayhi wa sallam) replied, "By preventing him from oppressing (others)."[24]

---

[24] Recorded by al-Bukhari. Book of Oppressions: chapter of: help your brother whether he is an oppressor or an oppressed. (2443-2444).

INTRODUCTION

This act of prevention is considered an assistance and Ihsaan to your Muslim brother/sister and you should keep in mind, when you deal with people, this Ayah,

$$\text{وَاللَّهُ يُحِبُّ الْمُحْسِنِينَ}$$

"**Allaah loves al-Muhsinun.**" In order to deal with people as good as possible.

Allaah says,

$$\text{وَالَّذِينَ إِذَا فَعَلُوا فَاحِشَةً أَوْ ظَلَمُوا أَنْفُسَهُمْ ذَكَرُوا اللَّهَ فَاسْتَغْفَرُوا لِذُنُوبِهِمْ}$$

"**And those who, when they have committed Fâhishah or wronged themselves with evil, remember Allaah and ask forgiveness for their sins.**" [25]

Al-Fâhishah: refers to repulsive and outrageous sins (i.e. major sins like adultery, drinking alcohol, and suicide ....etc.).

$$\text{أَوْ ظَلَمُوا أَنْفُسَهُمْ}$$

"**Wronged themselves with evil**"

Means: a lower degree than the Fâhishah (i.e. minor sins).

---

[25] Al-Imraan [3:135]

EXPLANATION OF RIYAADH SALIHEEN: THE CHAPTER ON HASTENING TO GOOD DEEDS

﴿ ذَكَرُوا اللَّهَ ﴾

"Remember Allaah"

Means: His majesty and His punishment, His mercy and acceptance of repentance and its subsequent reward. They remember Allaah from two aspects;

Firstly: they remember Allaah's majesty, punishment, and glorious dominance which inflicts fear, awe, and seeking forgiveness on their side.

Secondly: they remember Allaah's mercy and acceptance of repentance which arouse their desire for repentance and seeking forgiveness. Thus, Allaah says,

﴿ ذَكَرُوا اللَّهَ فَاسْتَغْفَرُوا لِذُنُوبِهِمْ ﴾

"they remember Allaah and ask forgiveness for their sins."

The best manner of seeking forgiveness is '**Syed-ul- Istighfaar**' to say,

اللَّهُمَّ أَنْتَ رَبِّي لَا إِلَهَ إِلَّا أَنْتَ، خَلَقْتَنِي وَ أَنَا عَبْدُكَ، وَ أَنَا عَلَى عَهْدِكَ وَ وَعْدِكَ مَا اسْتَطَعْتُ،

INTRODUCTION

أَعُوذُ بِكَ مِنْ شَرِّ مَا صَنَعْتُ، أَبُوءُ لَكَ بِنِعْمَتِكَ عَلَيَّ، وَ أَبُوءُ بِذَنْبِي فَاغْفِرْ لِي، فَإِنَّهُ لَا يَغْفِرُ الذُّنُوبَ إِلَّا أَنْتَ.

"O Allaah! You are my Lord. None has the right to be worshipped except You. You created me and I am your servant and I abide by your covenant and promise as best I can. I seek refuge in you from the evil, which I have committed. I acknowledge your favor upon me and I knowledge my sins, so forgive me, for verily none can forgive sin except you."[26]

Allaah says,

﴿وَمَن يَغْفِرُ ٱلذُّنُوبَ إِلَّا ٱللَّهُ﴾

"and none can forgive sins but Allaah"

If the entire Ummah, Jinn, and Angels were to assemble to forgive you for only one sin, they are powerless to do so because Allaah is the only that forgives and we should ask Allaah for forgiveness for us and those who preceded us in faith. Allaah says,

---

[26] Recorded by al-Bukhari. Book of supplications: chapter: the best of supplication: (6306).

EXPLANATION OF RIYAADH SALIHEEN: THE CHAPTER ON HASTENING TO GOOD DEEDS

﴿ وَلَمْ يُصِرُّوا۟ عَلَىٰ مَا فَعَلُوا۟ وَهُمْ يَعْلَمُونَ ﴾ ﴿١٣٥﴾

"And do not persist in what (wrong) they have done"

They don't persist because they are fully aware it is wrongdoing and oppression. This verse proves that persistence on committing the wrong, while knowing so, is grievous and this covers minor sins as well. This promoted plenty of scholars to maintain that persistence on committing a minor sin escalate its level to become a major one. For instance, what some ignorant people do nowadays of persistent beard-shaving and they think it's better-looking; whereas, it's actually shame and ugly because everything produced by the sin is stripped of goodness.

Those who persist on committing minor sins have mistaken because this persistence turn the minor sins to be major –Allaah forbid. Many of these people are heedless; whenever they go out to the market or their job, they check themselves on the mirror and if they found hair on the face, they rush to shave it- we ask Allaah to save us. This act is definitely disobedience to the prophet (salallahu 'alayhi wa sallam). In addition, there is a fear that Shaytān might gradually lead them to commit more grave and major sins. Allaah says,

INTRODUCTION

$$\text{﴿ أُوْلَٰٓئِكَ جَزَآؤُهُم مَّغْفِرَةٌ مِّن رَّبِّهِمْ وَجَنَّٰتٌ تَجْرِى مِن تَحْتِهَا ٱلْأَنْهَٰرُ خَٰلِدِينَ فِيهَا ۚ وَنِعْمَ أَجْرُ ٱلْعَٰمِلِينَ ﴾}$$

"For such, the reward is Forgiveness from their Lord, and Gardens with rivers flowing underneath (Paradise), wherein they shall abide forever. How excellent is this reward for the doers (who do righteous deeds according to Allâh's Orders)." [27]

O Allaah! Join us with those doers and make our reward the same as theirs.

---

[27] Al-Imraan [3:136]

EXPLANATION OF RIYAADH SALIHEEN: THE CHAPTER ON HASTENING TO GOOD DEEDS

HADITH NUMBER 87

٨٧- عَنْ أَبِي هُرَيْرَةَ رَضِيَ اللهُ عَنْهُ أَنَّ رَسُولَ الله - صَلَّى اللهُ عَلَيْهِ وَسَلَّمَ - قَالَ : ((بَادِرُوا بِالْأَعْمَالِ فِتَنًا كَقِطَعِ اللَّيْلِ الْمُظْلِمِ ، يُصْبِحُ الرَّجُلُ مُؤْمِنًا وَ يُمْسِي كَافِرًا، وَ يُمْسِي مُؤْمِنًا وَ يُصْبِحُ كَافِرًا، يَبِيعُ دِينَهُ بِعَرَضٍ مِنَ الدُّنْيَا)) رَوَاهُ مُسْلِمٌ.

87- Abu Hurairah reported that the Messenger of Allaah, may Allaah bless him and grant him peace, said, **"Hasten to actions during the times of Fitan (i.e. tribulations) which will be like patches of black night. A man will be a believer in the morning and an unbeliever in the evening, or a believer in the evening and an unbeliever in the morning. He will sell his Deen (religion) for the goods of this world."** [28] {Recorded by Muslim}

---

[28] Recorded by Muslim. Book of Emaan. Chapter of: Encouragement to hasten to do good deeds before the emergence of the Fitnah: (118).

HADITH NUMBER 87

The Explanation

The author 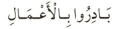 –rahimahullah- mentioned in what he narrated from the authority of Abu Hurairah- radiallahu 'anhu- that the prophet (salallahu 'alayhi wa sallam) said,

بَادِرُوا بِالْأَعْمَالِ

"Hasten to actions."

The intended meaning is the **'good'** deeds; good deeds have to fulfill two conditions: sincerity and adherence to the (Sunnah of) the prophet (salallahu 'alayhi wa sallam). This is the actual fulfillment of the testimony of: there is no God (worthy of worship) but Allaah and that Muhammad is His messenger.

The action that lacks the condition of sincerity is not considered as a good deed; if a person prays in order to show off, his/her prayer is not acceptable even if he/she fulfilled all of its conditions, pillars, requirements, its sunnan, tranquility, and outwardly perfected it, it isn't acceptable from him/her because it's mixed up with (minor) shirk (i.e. showing off) which nullifies any action as mentioned in the authentic Hadith narrated by Abu Hurairah that the prophet (salallahu 'alayhi wa sallam) said,

EXPLANATION OF RIYAADH SALIHEEN: THE CHAPTER ON HASTENING TO GOOD DEEDS

قَالَ اللهُ تَعَالَى : ((أَنَا أَغْنَى الشُّرَكَاءِ عَنِ الشِّرْكِ، مَنْ عَمِلَ عَمَلاً أَشْرَكَ فِيهِ مَعِي غَيْرِي تَرَكْتُهُ وَ شِرْكَهُ)) .

"Allaah (glorified and exalted be He) said: I am so self-sufficient that I am in no need of having an associate. Thus he who does an action for someone else's sake as well as Mine will have that action renounced by Me to him whom he associated with Me." [29]

Furthermore, the person may be sincere in his/her actions, but the method is inconsistent (Bid'ah) with what is legislated by the prophet ﷺ (salallahu 'alayhi wa sallam). The actions of the individual are not accepted even if he/she is sincere and weeps out of humility to Allaah, this won't benefit him/her because the Bid'ah (religious innovation) is described by the prophet ﷺ (sallahu 'alayhi wa sallam) as misguidance,

فَإِنَّ كُلَّ مُحْدَثَةٍ بِدْعَةٌ، وَ كُلَّ بِدْعَةٍ ضَلَالَةٌ

---

[29] Recorded by Muslim. Book of al-Zuhd: chapter: who associates others along with Allah in his/her actions: (2985).

HADITH NUMBER 87

"Every innovated matter (in Islam) is Bid'ah and every Bid'ah is misguidance."[30]

Then He said,

"Fitan (i.e. tribulations) which will be like patches of black night"

We seek refuge in Allaah- these tribulations will be extremely gloomy that completely block light- Allaah forbid. The person will be lost, confused, and doesn't know where to escape- I ask Allaah to save us from confusion. These tribulations arise due to either doubtful matters or (following one's) lusts. The fitan caused by doubtful matters are produced by ignorance as the case with those who innovated in their creed, sayings, and actions that which is not from the legislation of Allaah. The person may be tested by doubtful matters which alienate him/her from the truth- we seek refuge in Allaah from such things.

Similarly, transactions may involve some equivocal issues that don't confuse a certain

---

[30] Recorded by Abu Dawud. Book of Sunnah: chapter: adherence to the Sunnah: (4607), al-Tirmidhi. Book of al-Ilm: chapter of adherence to the Sunnah and avoidance of Bid'ah: (2676), ibn Majah in al-Muqadimmah: chapter of following the Sunnah of the rightly guided Caliphs: (42), and Ahmad in al-Musnad: (4/126-127). Al-Tirmidhi graded it as Hasan Sahih (sound and authentic).

EXPLANATION OF RIYAADH SALIHEEN: THE CHAPTER ON HASTENING TO GOOD DEEDS

person (who knows its rulings), but perplex a confused deviant- Allaah forbid. This deviant may be involved in a transaction he knew later it's forbidden; however, the rust on his heart caused by sins influences his decision and beautifies his bad deed that makes him eventually think it's good. Allaah says concerning this type of people,

"Say (O Muhammad Sallahu 'alayhi wa sallam): "Shall We tell you the greatest losers in respect of (their) deeds? (103) "Those whose efforts have been wasted in this life while they thought that they were acquiring good by their deeds!" [31]

They are the real losers- Allaah forbid.

Fitan also arise from lusts: meaning that the person knows that so and so is Haram, but he/she is heedless of doing it because his/her soul desires it. Similarly, he/she knows that so and so is obligatory, but his/her soul inclines to laziness and refrain from performing this obligation; this is the Fitnah of lust (i.e. following one's desires). Likewise, or rather the most

---

[31] Al-Kahf [18:103-104]

HADITH NUMBER 87

outrageous Fitnah is the lust of adultery and Homosexuality (i.e. sodomy) – Allaah forbid. These lusts considered among the most harmful diseases against the Ummah. The prophet (ﷺ) ('alayhi salātu wa sallam) said,

$$\text{مَا تَرَكْتُ بَعْدِي فِتْنَةً أَضَرَّ عَلَى الرِّجَالِ مِنَ النِّسَاءِ.}$$

"I have not left after me any (chance) of turmoil more injurious to men than the harm done to the men because of women." [32]

And He said,

$$\text{اتَّقُوا النِّسَاءَ، فَإِنَّ أَوَّلَ فِتْنَةِ بَنِي إِسْرَائِيلَ كَانَتْ فِي النِّسَاءِ.}$$

"Verily, the first trial for the people of Isra'il was caused by women." [33]

We have in our society nowadays who promotes this vice- Allaah forbid- with dishonest ways; they embellish their call with titles totally irrelevant to the essence of their call, but (titles)

---

[32] Recorded by al-Bukhari. Book of marriage: chapter: What evil omen of a lady is to be warded off: (5096), and Muslim. Book of heart-melting traditions: (2740).

[33] Recorded by Muslim. Book of heart-melting traditions: chapter: the majority of dwellers of the paradise are the poor, and the majority of the dwellers of the Hell-Fire is women (2742).

that serve their purpose such as exposing women and driving her out of her house to join men in their work. This brings about evil and turmoil; however, we ask Allah to ward off their deceit and to let a free hand to our rulers to expel them from anywhere they may potentially cause evil and corruption. In addition, we ask Allaah to grant our rulers righteous attendants who guide and urge them to all that is good.

The test of the people of Isra'il caused by women is the most harmful test. Some individuals in our contemporary time conspire to ruin woman's integrity in order to make her like a puppet designed to fulfill the lusts of dissipated and indecent human beings and to (fulfill) their desire of looking at her face anytime they want- we seek Allaah's refuge from such things. Nonetheless, by Allaah's might, the supplication of the Muslims (against them) will encompass them, suppress, and make them retreat unfruitful. The Saudi woman or rather Muslim women around the globe will be respected and protected wherever they are.

However, the prophet ﷺ ('alayhi salātu wa sallam) has warned against these trials that resemble the patches of gloomy night where the man is a believer in the morning and unbeliever in the evening- we seek refuge in Allaah. He apostates and become out of the fold of Islam in

HADITH NUMBER 87

one day- may Allaah save us-, but why is this? Because..

$$يَبِيعُ دِينَهُ بِعَرَضٍ مِنَ الدُّنْيَا$$

"He sells his Deen for the goods of this world"

Don't think this is just restricted to money rather it includes every temporal matter; wealth, prestige, presidency, women, and so on. Allaah says,

$$﴿ تَبْتَغُونَ عَرَضَ ٱلْحَيَوٰةِ ٱلدُّنْيَا فَعِندَ ٱللَّهِ مَغَانِمُ كَثِيرَةٌ ﴾$$

"seeking the perishable goods of the worldly life. There are much more profits and booties with Allaah." [34]

Those who are believers in the morning and unbelievers in the evening and vice-versa sell their religion for the goods of the Dunya- we ask Allaah to save all of us from Fitan (trials). Brothers! Always seek refuge from trials and how great that which the prophet (sallahu 'alayhi wa sallam) guided us to say,

$$إِذَا تَشَهَّدَ أَحَدُكُمْ فَلْيَسْتَعِذْ بِاللهِ مِنْ أَرْبَعٍ، يَقُولُ:$$
$$اللَّهُمَّ إِنِّي أَعُوذُ بِكَ مِنْ عَذَابِ جَهَنَّمَ، وَمِنْ$$

---

[34] Al-Nisā' [4:94]

EXPLANATION OF RIYAADH SALIHEEN: THE CHAPTER ON HASTENING TO GOOD DEEDS

عَذَابِ الْقَبْرِ، وَمِنْ فِتْنَةِ الْمَحْيَا وَالْمَمَاتِ، وَمِنْ شَرِّ فِتْنَةِ الْمَسِيحِ الدَّجَّالِ.

"When any one of you utters Tashahhud (in prayer) he must seek refuge with Allaah from four (trials) and should thus say: "O Allaah! I seek refuge with Thee from the torment of the Hell, from the torment of the grave, from the trial of life and death and from the evil of the trial of Masih al-Dajjaal (Antichrist)." [35]

We beseech Allaah to grant us firmness in this world and in the Hereafter upon the word (i.e. there is no God (worthy of worship) but Allaah, and that Muhammad is His messenger).

---

[35] Recorded by Muslim using this wording. Book of al-Masajid: chapter: things to be sought refuge against during prayer (588).

HADITH NUMBER 88

٨٨- عَنْ أَبِي سِرْوَعَةَ عُقْبَةَ ابْنِ الْحَارِثِ رَضِيَ اللهُ عَنْهُ قَالَ : صَلَّيْتُ وَرَاءَ النَّبِيِّ صَلَّى اللهُ عَلَيْهِ وَ سَلَّمَ بِالْمَدِينَةِ الْعَصْرَ ، فَسَلَّمَ ثُمَّ قَامَ مُسْرِعًا فَتَخَطَّى رِقَابَ النَّاسِ إِلَى بَعْضِ حُجَرِ نِسَائِهِ ، فَفَزِعَ النَّاسُ مِنْ سُرْعَتِهِ ، فَخَرَجَ عَلَيْهِمْ ، فَرَأَى أَنَّهُمْ قَدْ عَجِبُوا مِنْ سُرْعَتِهِ ، قَالَ : ((ذَكَرْتُ شَيْئًا مِنْ تِبْرٍ عِنْدَنَا ، فَكَرِهْتُ أَنْ يَحْبِسَنِي ، فَأَمَرْتُ بِقِسْمَتِهِ)) رَوَاهُ الْبُخَارِيّ.

وَ فِي رِوَايَةٍ لَهُ : ((كُنْتُ خَلَّفْتُ فِي الْبَيْتِ تِبْرًا مِنَ الصَّدَقَةِ ، فَكَرِهْتُ أَنْ أُبَيِّتَهُ)). ((التِّبْرُ)) قِطَعُ ذَهَبٍ أَوْ فِضَّةٍ .

88- Abu Sirwa'a 'Uqba ibn al-Harith said, "I prayed the 'Asr prayer behind the Prophet ﷺ (salallahu 'alayhi wa sallam) in Madina. He said the salam and then got up hurriedly and stepped over people's shoulders heading for the room of one of his wives. The people were alarmed at his speed. He came out to them and saw that they were surprised at his speed and said, 'I remembered a piece of gold that we had and I did not want it to distract me so I ordered that it be distributed.'"[36] [Al-Bukhari]

In another narration, "I had left a piece of gold from the sadaqah (charity) in the house and I did not want it to remain with me overnight."

The Explanation

This hadith promotes initiative for good deeds and the person should not be lazy in catching them because he/she is totally unaware when death strikes. The person should be shrewd (i.e. who dedicates his/her life for the purpose of the Hereafter) and avoid being careless; considering that the individual is attentive to matters related to the Dunya and seizes every possible opportunity, rather he/she should be likewise in matters of the Hereafter or even more (as it's worthier). Allaah says,

---

[36] - Recorded by al-Bukhari. Book of al-Adhaan: chapter: actions while praying: (851).

HADITH NUMBER 88

﴿ بَلْ تُؤْثِرُونَ ٱلْحَيَوٰةَ ٱلدُّنْيَا ۝ وَٱلْءَاخِرَةُ خَيْرٌ وَأَبْقَىٰ ۝ إِنَّ هَٰذَا لَفِى ٱلصُّحُفِ ٱلْأُولَىٰ ۝ صُحُفِ إِبْرَٰهِيمَ وَمُوسَىٰ ۝ ﴾

"Nay, you prefer the life of this world, (16) although the Hereafter is better and more lasting. (17) Verily, this is in the former Scriptures (18) The Scriptures of Ibrâhim (Abraham) and Mûsa (Moses)." [37]

This hadith indicates that the prophet ﷺ (salallahu 'alayhi wa sallam) is the fastest to do good deeds as he (salallahu 'alayhi wa sallam) in need for it as well as others. This is due to his statement,

إِنَّهُ لَنْ يَدْخُلَ الْجَنَّةَ أَحَدٌ بِعَمَلِهِ، قَالُوا : وَلَا أَنْتَ ؟ قَالَ : ((وَلَا أَنَا إِلَّا أَنْ يَتَغَمَّدَنِيَ اللهُ بِرَحْمَتِهِ)).

"one's good deeds will not make him enter Paradise." They asked, "Even you, O Allaah's Messenger (salallahu 'alayhi wa sallam)?" He said, "Even me, unless and until Allaah bestows His pardon and Mercy on me." [38]

---

[37] al-Ala [87:16-19]
[38] Recorded by al-Bukhārī. Book of heart-melting traditions. Chapter: The adoption of a middle course, and the regularity of deeds (6463), and Muslim. Book of description of the Day of

EXPLANATION OF RIYAADH SALIHEEN: THE CHAPTER ON HASTENING TO GOOD DEEDS

And he is the prophet ﷺ ('alayhi salātu wa sallam).

This hadith proves the permissibility of stepping over shoulders after the final Salam in prayer especially for necessity because people after Salah are not required to stay where they prayed, but to leave. This is opposed to stepping over shoulders before the beginning of the prayer which is impermissible because it annoys people. Therefore, the prophet ﷺ (salallahu 'alayhi wa sallam) cut off his Khutbah on Friday when he saw a man stepping over people's shoulders and instructed him to,

اجْلِسْ فَقَدْ آذَيْتَ

"Sit, you have annoyed the people."[39]

This hadith also proves that the prophet ﷺ (salallahu 'alayhi wa sallam) is similar to his fellow human beings in terms of forgetting and since he forgets what he has already known, it's obvious that he is unaware of what he does not know as Allaah told him,

---

Judgment. Chapter: one's good deeds will not make him enter Paradise (2816).
[39] Recorded by Abu Dawud. Book of Salah. Chapter: stepping over people's shoulders on Friday (1118), al-Nasā'ī: Book of Jumu'ah. Chapter: the impermissibility of stepping over people's shoulders (1399), and Ibn Hiban in his Sahih (572).

HADITH NUMBER 88

> ﴿ قُل لَّا أَقُولُ لَكُمْ عِندِى خَزَآئِنُ ٱللَّهِ وَلَآ أَعْلَمُ ٱلْغَيْبَ وَلَآ أَقُولُ لَكُمْ إِنِّى مَلَكٌ ﴾

"Say (O Muhammad salallahu 'alayhi wa sallam): "I don't tell you that with me are the treasures of Allaah, nor (that) I know the unseen; nor I tell you that I am an angel." [40]

Allaah has ordered him to publically declare that he does not possess the treasures of Allaah, nor knows the unseen, nor an angel (Salwatullahi wa Salaamuhu 'alayhi).

This hadith blocks all possible paths against those who resort to the prophet ﷺ (sallahu 'alayhi wa sallam) in times of distress and call upon him; verily, they are his enemies not his followers and if he were to be alive, he would ask them to repent otherwise he would kill them if they refused because they are polytheists. The person must not call upon other than Allaah such as a close angel, nor a messenger. The prophet ﷺ (sallahu 'alayhi wa sallam) was sent to safeguard Tawheed (Monotheism) and to put Allaah's worship into action. The prophet ﷺ (salallahu 'alayhi wa sallam) does not know the unseen and sometimes forgets what he knows, he is in need for food, drink, clothes, and protection against enemies. In addition, he

---

[40] Al-An'aam [6:50]

EXPLANATION OF RIYAADH SALIHEEN: THE CHAPTER ON HASTENING TO GOOD DEEDS

(sallahu 'alayhi wa sallam) protected himself with two shields in Ghazwah (military expedition) Uhud out of fear of the sword.

The prophet 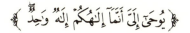 (sallahu 'alayhi wa sallam) is identical to other human beings in terms of sharing the same features of the human race. Allaah says,

﴿ قُلْ إِنَّمَآ أَنَا۠ بَشَرٌ مِّثْلُكُمْ يُوحَىٰٓ إِلَىَّ أَنَّمَآ إِلَٰهُكُمْ إِلَٰهٌ وَٰحِدٌ ﴾

"Say (O Muhammad salallahu 'alayhi wa sallam): "I am only a man like you. It has been revealed to me that your Ilâh (God) is One Ilâh (God — i.e. Allaah)." [41]

Observe describing him as a human being **'like you'**. If 'like you' has not been mentioned, it would have sufficed (i.e. we knew that he is a human being by means of analogy), but Allaah says **'like you'** to imply that the only distinction between the prophet and the human being is the revelation,

﴿ يُوحَىٰٓ إِلَىَّ أَنَّمَآ إِلَٰهُكُمْ إِلَٰهٌ وَٰحِدٌ ﴾

"It has been revealed to me that your Ilâh (God) is One Ilâh (God — i.e. Allaah)"

This hadith emphasizes the significance of trust (al-'Amânah) and that the person should hasten

---

[41] Al-Kahf [18:110]

HADITH NUMBER 88

to deliver it (to its owner) otherwise it might disturb him/her and thereby the prophet said,

فَكَرِهْتُ أَنْ يَحْبِسَنِي

"I did not want it to distract me."

The person should also hasten to repay his/her debt as well as delivering the trust. One must repay his/her debt if it's due otherwise delaying it is permissible if the creditor allowed it. Scholars- rahimahumallah- maintained: the obligation of pilgrimage is waived for the sake of whoever in debt until the debt is repaid because the matter of debt is very critical.

The prophet ﷺ ('alayhi salātu wa sallam) before conquests used to inquire about the dead person for whom he will lead the funeral prayer; if he is indebted, he won't pray unless the dead person has what covers his/her debt. The prophet did not lead the funeral prayer of the person died indebted; one day a dead man from al-Ansar was brought before the prophet to offer the funeral prayer. The prophet asked, **"Is he indebted?"** the response was: Yes, he has a debt of three Dinars but he doesn't have what covers it. The prophet (sallahu 'alayhi wa sallam) refused to lead the prayer and ordered his friends to lead the funeral prayer (instead of him). This negative response had a remarkable impact on the people witnessing the situation wandering: How hasn't the prophet (salallahu

EXPLANATION OF RIYAADH SALIHEEN: THE CHAPTER ON HASTENING TO GOOD DEEDS

'alayhi wa sallam) lead the prayer?! Abu Qatadah –radiallahu 'anhu- approached the prophet and told him: I undertake his debt and thereby the prophet ﷺ (sallahu 'alayhi wa sallam) acceded to lead the prayer.[42]

Unfortunately, you find many indebted people while they are financially able to repay it but they procrastinate its payment- we seek refuge in Allaah. It has been authentically narrated that the prophet 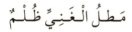 ('alayhi salātu wa sallam) said,

مَطْلُ الْغَنِيِّ ظُلْمٌ

"Delay in payment by a rich man is injustice."[43]

Know that debt is misunderstood by (some) people since they think that debt is that when a person buys goods with an expensive price than its actual price. Rather, debt is whatever the person is liable to pay such as loans, house rent, or even the car fare. The person must hasten to repay his/her debt whenever it's due.

---

[42] Recorded by al-Bukhari. Book of al-Hiwalah (Transference): chapter: If the debts due on a dead person are transferred to somebody, the transference is legal (2289).
[43] Recorded by al-Bukhari. Book of Transference. Chapter: Al-Hawala (the transference of a debt from one person to another) (2287), and Muslim, book of transactions, chapter: the forbiddance of debt delay from a rich person (1564).

HADITH NUMBER 88

Moreover, this hadith proves the permissibility of authorizing somebody else to distribute whatever the person is liable to distribute. The prophet said,

$$فَأَمَرْتُ بِقِسْمَتِهِ$$

"I ordered it to be distributed."

This permissible authorization (for others on one's behalf) applies for any issue related to Allaah's right such as pilgrimage, alms-giving and human rights like buying, selling, mortgage, and so on.

The conclusion: This hadith prompts people to have the initiative for good deeds and to avoid laziness in doing so. You should take in consideration that the one's soul adapts to whatever he/she habituates it to do; be it determination and initiation or laziness and slackness. I ask Allaah (Gory be to Him) to aid us remembering Him, expressing our gratitude to Him, and to worship Him in the best manner.

EXPLANATION OF RIYAADH SALIHEEN: THE CHAPTER ON HASTENING TO GOOD DEEDS

HADITH NUMBER 89

٨٩- عَنْ جَابِرٍ رَضِيَ اللهُ عَنْهُ قَالَ : قَالَ رَجُلٌ لِلنَّبِيِّ صَلَّى اللهُ عَلَيْهِ وَسَلَّمَ يَوْمَ أُحُدٍ : أَرَأَيْتَ إِنْ قُتِلْتُ فَأَيْنَ أَنَا ؟ قَالَ : ((فِي الْجَنَّةِ)) فَأَلْقَى تَمَرَاتٍ كُنَّ فِي يَدِهِ ، ثُمَّ قَاتَلَ حَتَّى قُتِلَ . مُتَّفَقٌ عَلَيْهِ

89- Jabir said, "A man said to the Prophet (sallahu 'alayhi wa sallam) on the day of Uhud, 'Where do you think that I will be if I am killed?' He said, 'In the paradise.' Immediately thereafter he threw away some dates that were in his hand and then fought until he was killed.'[44] {Agreed upon}

The Explanation

This hadith points out the initiative of the companions for good deeds –radiallahu 'anhum- and that they never procrastinate as it is their attitude which inherited them honor on this life

---

[44] Recorded by al-Bukhari, book of al-Maghaazi (the expeditions), chapter of Ghazwat Uhud (4046), and Muslim, book of rulership, chapter: paradise is the dweller of martyrs (1899).

HADITH NUMBER 89

and the next to come. Similarly, the prophet ﷺ (sallahu 'alayhi wa sallam) delivered a speech on the day of Eid (festival), then addressed the women and commanded them to give Sadaqah (charity). In return, the women took off their earrings and rings and put them in the garment of Bilal, who was collecting, and he gave them to the prophet[45] ﷺ (salallahu 'alayhi wa sallam). Those women- radiallahu 'anhu- were highly responsive to give charity even from their own jewelry.

The hadith of Jabir contains many benefits:

1- Whoever is killed for the sake of Allaah will be resided in the paradise, but for whom this description befits? It befits whoever fights in order for the Word of Allaah to be the topmost as opposed to whoever fights for the sake of fanaticism, bravery, or showing off; rather he is fighting only for the Word of Allaah to be the topmost. As for those who fight out of fanaticism like those who fight for the sake of Arabian nationalism not for the sake of Allaah.

2- Whoever fights out of bravery: is that whose bravery prompts him to fight (i.e. in order to exhibit it before himself). Most often, the person likes to express any trait he/she is

---

[45] Recorded by al-Bukhari, book of Zakah, chapter: encouraging charity (1431), and Muslim, book of al-'Eidain, chapter: the Salah of al-Eidain (884).

characterized with. This individual, if he is killed, is not considered for the sake of Allaah.

Whoever fights to show off- we seek Allaah's refuge- and be publicly observed during his battle against the disbelievers. This is not for the sake of Allaah because the prophet ﷺ (salallahu 'alayhi wa sallam) was asked about the man who fights out of bravery, a man who fights to defend himself and a man who fights to show off, and whether any of these were fighting in the way of Allaah The Messenger of Allaah (sallahu 'alayhi wa sallam) said,

مَنْ قَاتَلَ لِتَكُونَ كَلِمَةُ اللهِ هِيَ الْعُلْيَا فَهُوَ فِي سَبِيلِ اللهِ.

"The one fights so that the word of Allaah will be topmost is in the way of Allaah."

This hadith proves that the companions are very diligent in seeking knowledge because this man asked the prophet ﷺ ('alayhi salātu wa sallam) about matters of their traditions. They don't waste any chance where they can ask the prophet ﷺ (salallahu 'alayhi wa sallam) due to the benefit they gain in knowledge and in their practical life. The knowledge bestowed upon a scholar is a favor from Allaah and this

HADITH NUMBER 89

favor is doubled if Allaah guides him to implement this knowledge.

This was the attitude of the companions – radiallahu 'anhum- to ask the prophet ﷺ (salallahu 'alayhi wa sallam) about the legal rulings in order to implement them by contrast with the situation nowadays to many people. Those people ask about legal rulings and when they're well-informed about them, they abandon and completely discard them as if they seek knowledge for just the theoretical side; actually, this is a manifest loss because who abandons implementing knowledge after knowing it is worse than the ignorant.

If someone wandered: would we judge, those who claim to fight for the sake of Islam and to defend it, as martyrs if they died? The answer is: No, we don't acknowledge that they are martyrs because the prophet ﷺ (salallahu 'alayhi wa sallam) said,

مَا مِنْ مَكْلُومٍ يُكْلَمُ فِي سَبِيلِ اللهِ - وَ اللهُ أَعْلَمُ بِمَنْ يُكْلَمُ فِي سَبِيلِهِ - إِلَّا جَاءَ يَوْمَ الْقِيَامَةِ وَ جُرْحُهُ يَثْعَبُ دَمًا، اللَّوْنُ لَوْنُ الدَّمِ، وَ الرِّيحُ رِيحُ الْمِسْكِ

"No one is wounded in the cause of Allaah - and Allaah knows best who is

EXPLANATION OF RIYAADH SALIHEEN: THE CHAPTER ON HASTENING TO GOOD DEEDS

wounded in His cause - but he will come on the Day of Resurrection with his wounds bleeding the color of blood, but with the fragrance of musk."[46]

The prophet's statement,

وَاللهُ أَعْلَمُ بِمَنْ يُكْلَمُ فِي سَبِيلِهِ

"Allaah knows best who is wounded in His cause." signifies that it revolves around the intention hidden from us while known to Allaah. Umar ibn al-Khattab delivered a speech one day in which he said: You call so and so a martyr while that (so and so) may have stolen his riding camel. Don't say this but say: **'whoever'** died or killed for the sake of Allaah is a martyr. Don't testify to a **'particular'** person that he is a martyr except for whom Allaah and His messenger have testified he is a martyr. As for other than this type (i.e. for whom Allaah and His messenger testified) generalize your statement; whoever is killed for the sake of Allaah is a martyr and we wish for him to be included among them. And Allaah is the one who grants success.

---

[46] Recorded by al-Bukhari, book of Jihad, chapter: who fights for the sake of Allaah (2803), and Muslim, book of al-Imarah, chapter: the virtue of Jihad and fighting for the sake of Allaah (1876).

HADITH NUMBER 90

٩٠- عَنْ أَبِي هُرَيْرَةَ -رَضِيَ اللهُ عَنْهُ- قَالَ: جَاءَ رَجُلٌ إِلَى النَّبِيِّ صَلَّى اللهُ عَلَيْهِ وَ سَلَّمَ، فَقَالَ: يَا رَسُولَ الله. أَيُّ الصَّدَقَةِ أَعْظَمُ أَجْرًا؟ قَالَ: ((أَنْ تَصَدَّقَ وَ أَنْتَ صَحِيحٌ شَحِيحٌ تَخْشَى الْفَقْرَ، وَتَأْمُلُ الْغِنَى، وَلَا تُمْهِلْ حَتَّى إِذَا بَلَغَتِ الْحُلْقُومَ قُلْتَ لِفُلَانٍ كَذَا وَلِفُلَانٍ كَذَا، وَ قَدْ كَانَ لِفُلَانٍ)). مُتَّفَقٌ عَلَيْهِ.

90- Abu Hurayrah said, "A man came to the Prophet (salallahu 'alayhi wa sallam) and said, 'O Messenger of Allaah, which sadaqah has the greatest reward?' He said, 'The sadaqah that you give when you are healthy but tight-fisted, in fear of poverty and desiring wealth. Do not put it off until the soul reaches the throat (i.e. sign of death) and you say, "So-and-so should have this much and so-and-so this much,"' when it already belongs to someone else."[47] [Agreed upon]

The Explanation

---

[47] Recorded by al-Bukhari, book of Zakah, chapter: the virtue of charity of a healthy miser person (1419), and Muslim, book of Zakah: The best of charity is that which is given when one is a healthy miser person (1032).

EXPLANATION OF RIYAADH SALIHEEN: THE CHAPTER ON HASTENING TO GOOD DEEDS

This hadith is listed under the chapter of: Initiative for good deeds and performing them without hesitation. The hadith (states) that a man asked the prophet (salallahu 'alayhi wa sallam) about which Sadaqah has the greatest reward? The questionnaire does not refer to the type or the amount of Sadaqah but refers to the best timing of giving out Sadaqah when nothing is comparable to it. The prophet (salallahu 'alayhi wa sallam) answered: to give out charity when you're healthy and tight-fisted.

Healthy highlights the physical health while tight-fisted highlights one's trait. The individual tends to be tight-fisted when he/she is entertaining a good health because he/she wishes long-life time and fears poverty. Whereas, if the person is sick, Dunya is worthless and it becomes easier for him/her to give out Sadaqah. The prophet said,

أَنْ تَصَدَّقَ وَأَنْتَ صَحِيحٌ شَحِيحٌ تَخْشَى الْفَقْرَ

"To give out Sadaqah while you are healthy and tight-fisted in fear of poverty and desiring a long-life"

and in another narration,

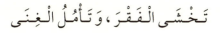

HADITH NUMBER 90

"in fear of poverty and desiring wealth."

The first narration is better because **"desiring a long-life"** befits when the individual is healthy and wishful for long life because the healthy person excludes death although it might suddenly strikes; as opposed to the sick person who thinks of death as imminent. The statement of **"fear of poverty"** arises from the long life because people fear poverty over their life since everything one has runs out. Therefore, this is the best thing one should do; to give out Sadaqah when you are healthy and tight-fisted.

"Don't put it off"

Meaning: the Sadaqah.

حَتَّى إِذَا بَلَغَتِ الْحُلْقُومَ قُلْتَ لِفُلَانٍ كَذَا وَلِفُلَانٍ كَذَا، وَقَدْ كَانَ لِفُلَانٍ

"until death is near and you say, "So-and-so should have this much and so-and-so this much,"

and after you become certain of your death and saying "this so and so should have this much and that so and so should have this much" of Sadaqah while it already belongs to someone else (i.e. his/her inheritors) as one's property is automatically transferred to the inheritors. This hadith encourages the individual to seize this chance before death and gives out Sadaqah. If he/she were to give out Sadaqah during the agonies of death, it would be less in reward than giving it out when the person is healthy and tight-fisted.

This hadith implies a proof that the person's speech is considered (valid) near death time before he/she becomes unconscious of his/her speech; by then, the speech is not considered to be valid due to the prophet's statement,

حَتَّى إِذَا بَلَغَتِ الْحُلْقُومَ قُلْتَ لِفُلَانٍ كَذَا وَلِفُلَانٍ كَذَا، وَقَدْ كَانَ لِفُلَانٍ

"until the soul reaches the throat (i.e. sign of death) and you say, "So-and-so should have this much and so-and-so this much,"" when it already belongs to someone else."

It proves that the soul comes out from the lower part of the body and goes up to the top where it's taken as a sign for a person's death, **"reaches the throat."** This is similar to Allaah's saying,

﴿ فَلَوْلَا إِذَا بَلَغَتِ الْحُلْقُومَ ۝ وَأَنتُمْ حِينَئِذٍ تَنظُرُونَ ۝ ﴾

HADITH NUMBER 90

"Then why do you not (intervene) when (the soul of a dying person) reaches the throat? (83) And you at the moment are looking on." [48]

The lower part of the body is the first that dies where the soul goes up the body until it reaches the throat and then the angel of death takes it. We ask Allaah to end our life with good and happiness. Allaah is the one that grants success.

[48] Al-Waqi'ah [56:83-84]

EXPLANATION OF RIYAADH SALIHEEN: THE CHAPTER ON HASTENING TO GOOD DEEDS

HADITH NUMBER 91

٩١- عَنْ أَنَسٍ رَضِيَ اللهُ عَنْهُ، أَنَّ رَسُولَ اللهِ صَلَّى اللهُ عَلَيْهِ وَ سَلَّمَ أَخَذَ سَيْفًا يَوْمَ أُحُدٍ فَقَالَ : ((مَنْ يَأْخُذُ مِنِّي هَذَا؟ فَبَسَطُوا أَيْدِيَهُمْ، كُلُّ إِنْسَانٍ مِنْهُمْ يَقُولُ : أَنَا أَنَا . قَالَ : ((فَمَنْ يَأْخُذُ بِحَقِّهِ؟)) فَاحْجَمَ الْقَوْمُ، فَقَالَ أَبُو دُجَانَةَ رَضِيَ اللهُ عَنْهُ: أَنَا آخُذُهُ بِحَقِّهِ، فَأَخَذَهُ فَفَلَقَ بِهِ هَامَ الْمُشْرِكِينَ . رَوَاهُ مُسْلِمٌ .

91- Anas reported that the Messenger of Allah took a sword on the day of Uhud and said, "Who will take this from me?" They stretched out their hands, every man of them, saying, "Me! Me!" He said, "Who will take it with its right?" The people held back. Abu Dujana said, "I will take it with its right." He took it and split open the heads of the idolaters with it. [Muslim][49]

The name of Abu Dujana is: Samak ibn Kharshah.

---

[49] Recorded by Muslim, book of the virtues of the companions, chapter: virtues of Abu Dujana (2470).

HADITH NUMBER 91

The Explanation

Anas narrated this hadith about (an incident) during the expedition of Uhud[50], one of the most significant expeditions led by the prophet ﷺ (salallahu 'alayhi wa sallam) himself. The cause of this Ghazwah: the tribe of Quraish wanted to take revenge after their loss in the battle of Badr where their leaders have been killed. Therefore, they set out heading for al-Madinah to fight the prophet ﷺ (salallahu 'alayhi wa sallam) who, in return, consulted his companions after he knew they're coming. Some of them preferred to stay and fight in al-Madinah as they would be (strategically) in a good position to shower them with arrows while being fortified in their houses.

Others suggested, especially the youth who hadn't attended the battle of Badr, to fight outside al-Madinah. Thereafter, the prophet ﷺ (salallahu 'alayhi wa sallam) entered his house and dressed up with war cloth then went out and ordered for the battle to be outside al-Madinah in the battle of Uhud. They faced the disbelievers in Uhud and the prophet ﷺ (salallahu 'alayhi wa sallam) lined up his troops perfectly, put the archers (50) in the top of the mountain led by Abdullah ibn Jubayer- radiallahu 'anhu-. He instructed them not to

---

[50] Uhud: is a mountain located near to al-Madinah.

leave the mountain and remain there whether Muslims were winning or losing.

In the beginning of the battle, the disbelievers were starting to lose and retreating. Muslims, then, started to collect the booty and the archers on the top of the mountain said: let's come down and collect the booty, but their leader reminded them of the prophet's orders to remain on the mountain even if the Muslims are winning.

However, they –radiallahu 'anhum- thought it's all over because they witnessed the retreat of the disbelievers except some of them who were still there. Thereupon, the knights of the disbelievers attacked Muslims from the back after they saw the mountain almost empty from (Muslim) archers. They mixed up with the Muslim army and everything happened accordingly to what Allaah has decreed. Muslims' casualties were 70 martyrs (and most prominently) Hamza- radiallahu 'anhu- the lion of Allaah and His messenger and the paternal uncle of the prophet ﷺ - salallahu 'alayhi wa sallam.

Muslims expressed their shock after this gigantic distress: how is that?! How did we lose and the prophet ﷺ (salallahu 'alayhi wa sallam) is with us and we are the soldiers of Allaah while the disbelievers are allies with the devils and they are the soldiers of Satan? Allaah says,

HADITH NUMBER 91

$$\{ أَوَلَمَّا أَصَابَتْكُم مُّصِيبَةٌ قَدْ أَصَبْتُم مِّثْلَيْهَا قُلْتُمْ أَنَّىٰ هَٰذَا ۖ قُلْ هُوَ مِنْ عِندِ أَنفُسِكُمْ \}$$

"(What is the matter with you?) When a single disaster smites you, although you smote (your enemies) with one twice as great, you say: "From where does this come to us?" Say (to them), "It is from yourselves (because of your evil deeds)." 51

The loss is because of your sins as in Allaah's saying,

$$\{ حَتَّىٰ إِذَا فَشِلْتُمْ وَتَنَازَعْتُمْ فِي الْأَمْرِ وَعَصَيْتُم مِّن بَعْدِ مَا أَرَاكُم مَّا تُحِبُّونَ \}$$

"until (the moment) you lost your courage and fell to disputing about the order, and disobeyed after He showed you (of the booty) which you love." 52

Then happened what you hate to happen.

Muslims lost in this battle for sublime purposes mentioned in Surat Al-Imran and expounded by al-Hafiz Ibn Al-Qayyim –rahimahullah- in his book "Zaad al-Ma'ad" in an impressive manner I have never read similar to it. He explained the

---

51 Al-Imran [3:165]
52 Al-Imran [3:152]

sublime purposes derived from this battle (of Uhud).

Back to the hadith, the prophet ﷺ (salallahu 'alayhi wa sallam) took a sword and told his companions, **"Who will take this sword?"** All of them wanted to take it; they put their hands out and stretched them (to take it). The prophet ﷺ (salallahu 'alayhi wa sallam), **"Who will take it with its right?"** they withdrew because they don't know what is the right of it and (also) being afraid they won't be able to undertake this right if it's beyond their capacity, which would break the fulfillment of the promise they gave to the prophet if they took the sword.

However, Allaah favored Abu Dujana –radiallahu 'anhu- who agreed to take the sword with its right (i.e. that he should take and strike with it until it's broken). He- radiallahu anhu- took it, fought with it, and split open the heads of the polytheists. This proves that the person should hasten to do good deeds and never puts if off while seeking Allaah's assistance. Allaah, in return, would assist him/her if this person rightly sought His assistance and completely trusted Him.

Many people may deem acts of worship as excessive or difficult to perform which leads them to retreat; instead, it should be said to

HADITH NUMBER 91

them: seek Allaah's assistance and have reliance on Allaah and if you were to do so and engage in what pleases Him, be sure of good tidings that Allaah would assist you as He says,

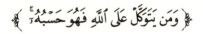

"And whosoever puts his trust in Allaah, then He will suffice him." [53]

This hadith also emphasizes on the prophet's great care over his Ummah because he hasn't specified anyone to take the sword but rather he left it open for anyone to take it; this should be the behavior towards the subjects of anyone whom Allaah has entrusted. He/she should not be biased or even act in a manner that seems to involve bias because if he/she do so, disunity is the outcome that negatively affect the unity of the group. But if there is a distinguished person and he/she was favored due to his/her distinguishing trait not found in others, while it's clear why he is favored, then there is no harm and Allaah is the one who grants success.

---

[53] At-Talaq [65:3]

EXPLANATION OF RIYAADH SALIHEEN: THE CHAPTER ON HASTENING TO GOOD DEEDS

HADITH NUMBER 92

٩٢- عَنِ الزُّبَيْرِ بْنِ عَدِيٍّ قَالَ: أَتَيْنَا أَنَسَ بْنَ مَالِكٍ - رَضِيَ اللهُ عَنْهُ - فَشَكَوْنَا إِلَيْهِ مَا نَلْقَى مِنَ الْحَجَّاجِ. فَقَالَ: ((اِصْبِرُوا، فَإِنَّهُ لَا يَأْتِي عَلَيْكُمْ زَمَانٌ إِلَّا وَ الَّذِي بَعْدَهُ شَرٌّ مِنْهُ حَتَّى تَلْقَوْا رَبَّكُمْ)) سَمِعْتُهُ مِنْ نَبِيِّكُمْ صَلَّى اللهُ عَلَيْهِ وَ سَلَّمَ. رَوَاهُ الْبُخَارِي.

Az-Zubayr ibn 'Adi narrated, "We went to Anas ibn Malik –radiallahu 'anhu- and complained to him about what we are we suffering on the part of al-Hajjaj. He said, 'Be patient. There is no time will come but the time following it will be worse than it until you meet your Lord.' I heard that from your Prophet."[54] **[Al-Bukhari]**

The Explanation

The author –rahimahullah- recorded what Az-Zubayr ibn 'Adi narrated that they went to Anas ibn Malik, - radiallahu 'anhu- the servant of the

---

[54] Recorded by al-Bukhari, book of Fitan, chapter: no time will come but the one following it will be worse than it (7068).

HADITH NUMBER 92

prophet (salallahu 'alayhi wa sallam). He had been aged until he died around the eightieth year of Hijrah in which he experienced some of Fitan that befell upon Muslims. Those people came to him complaining (the ruthless) of al-Hajjaj ibn Yusuf al-Thaqafy, one of the Umayyad's rulers and he was known to be an oppressor, a shedder of blood, tyrannical, and stubborn- we seek Allaah's refuge. He is the one who besieged Makkah in order to fight Abdullah ibn Az-Zubair –radiallahu 'anhu- and stoned the ka'bah using catapult until he destroyed it or destroyed some of it. He inflicted an (unbearable) harm against his subjects.

Therefore, they were complaining to Anas ibn Malik –radiallahu 'anhu- and he instructed them to have patience in the face of tyranny of rulers because rulers may be a punishment for their subjects due to the subjects' sins. Allaah says,

$$﴿ وَكَذَٰلِكَ نُوَلِّي بَعْضَ ٱلظَّٰلِمِينَ بَعْضًۢا بِمَا كَانُوا۟ يَكْسِبُونَ ﴾$$

"And thus We do make the Zâlimûn (polytheists and wrongdoers, etc.) Auliyâ (supporters and helpers) one to another (in committing crimes etc.), because of that which they used to earn." [55]

So, when rulers swindle the subjects in their wealth, inflict physical harm, hinder between the

---

[55] Al-'An'aam [7:129]

EXPLANATION OF RIYAADH SALIHEEN: THE CHAPTER ON HASTENING TO GOOD DEEDS

callers and Da'wah to Allaah (Glory be to Him) and whatever is similar to this, consider the subjects' condition; you would find that affliction is caused by the subjects as they're the ones deviated and subsequently Allaah punished them with (tyrant) rulers. It's mentioned in al-'Athar –not a hadith-: your rulers reflect your condition.

It's reported that one of the Umayyad rulers – I think he is Abdul Malik ibn Marwan- held a meeting with notable people of the society when he was learnt about the talk of the people about rulership. He gathered those notable people and asked them: O people! Do you want us to be rulers like Abu Bakr and Umar? They answered: yes, we do. He replied: then you should be like the subjects (i.e. citizens) ruled by Abu Bakr and Umar in order for us to be as them. This means that rulers reflect the condition of the people; if the rulers are oppressors, it's, most often, due to the sins of their subjects.

A man from al-Khawarij (rebellions) came to Ali ibn Abi Talib –radiallahu 'anhu- and asked him: what's the matter with the people repelled against you while they had not done with Abu Bakr and Umar. He answered: Because, the subjects of Abu Bakr and Umar are like me and the likes of me, while my subjects are you and the likes of you. It means that if the subjects are

HADITH NUMBER 92

themselves oppressor, they are punished by their rulers.

For this reason, Anas said: Be patient. This instruction with patience is essential since every distress shall be dispelled. Don't think that everything will come easy; evil might suddenly strikes but it will never be triumphant over goodness. We should be patient, be wise, and never surrender nor become rash. We should employ wisdom, patience, and deliberation when we deal with life matters. Allaah says,

﴿ يَٰٓأَيُّهَا ٱلَّذِينَ ءَامَنُوا۟ ٱصْبِرُوا۟ وَصَابِرُوا۟ وَرَابِطُوا۟ وَٱتَّقُوا۟ ٱللَّهَ لَعَلَّكُمْ تُفْلِحُونَ ۝ ﴾

"O you who believe! Endure and be more patient (than your enemy), and guard your territory by stationing army units permanently at the places from where the enemy can attack you, and fear Allaah, so that you may be successful." [56]

If you pursue successfulness, then these are its means and causes mentioned earlier in the ayah.

Anas ibn Malik then said,

"There will no time but the one following it will be worse than it until you meet your Lord. I heard it from your prophet

---
[56] Al-Imran [3:200]

EXPLANATION OF RIYAADH SALIHEEN: THE CHAPTER ON HASTENING TO GOOD DEEDS

Muhammad (salallahu 'alayhi wa sallam)."

It will religiously become more evil[57] but it's not an absolute evil; rather it may be more evil in some respects and better in other respects.

Nonetheless, as deeper people are getting immersed in indulgence and become open up as more evil will unfold. Indulgence destroys the individual because if the individual pursues indulgence and excessive comfort, he/she will overlook flourishing his/her heart and become increasingly concerned to afford comfort for the physical body which eventually decomposes and (eaten) by earthworms.

This is the real affliction and this is what harms people nowadays. You find people saying: our palace, our car, our furniture, and our food is so and so even those who are concerned with knowledge and study it; some of them study for the sake of being awarded with a rank that facilitates worldly benefits for him/her. It looks as if the person was not created for a great purpose while the Dunya and its benefits are just serving that great purpose (i.e. worshipping Allaah). We ask Allaah to make the Dunya a mean for us to (attain His pleasure).

---

[57] **Translator's note:** The author means that religious strictness will be getting loose as time goes. This looseness brings about evil which evolves over time and is relatively dependent on how far are people away from the religion.

HADITH NUMBER 92

Shaykhul al-Islam ibn Taymiyah –rahimahullah- said, "The individual should use money as he/she uses the donkey for riding and the bathroom for discharging excrement." Or he said something similar to that.

Those (who follow that) know exactly what money is and its actual value. Avoid making money your biggest concern. You should have a grip over the money otherwise it will overwhelm you and you would become wholly pre-occupied by Dunya. Thus, we maintain that as much indulgence and engaging people are experiencing of Dunya (benefits), as much loss of the Hereafter they will suffer. The prophet ﷺ (salallahu 'alayhi wa sallam) said,

وَاللهِ مَا الْفَقْرَ أَخْشَى عَلَيْكُمْ، وَلَكِنِّي أَخْشَى أَنْ تُبْسَطَ عَلَيْكُمُ الدُّنْيَا كَمَا بُسِطَتْ عَلَى مَنْ كَانَ قَبْلَكُمْ، فَتَنَافَسُوهَا كَمَا تَنَافَسُوهَا، وَتُهْلِكَكُمْ كَمَا أَهْلَكَتْهُمْ.

"**By Allaah, I am not afraid that you will be poor, but I fear that worldly wealth will be bestowed upon you as it was bestowed upon those who lived before you. So you will compete amongst yourselves for it, as they competed for it**

EXPLANATION OF RIYAADH SALIHEEN: THE
CHAPTER ON HASTENING TO GOOD DEEDS

and it will destroy you as it did with them."[58]

The prophet ﷺ (salallahu alayhi wa sallam) has been truthful. This is what destroyed people nowadays; competing for the Dunya and acting as if they were created for it not as if it's created for them. This led them to be pre-occupied with what is created for them instead of being pre-occupied with what they are created for (i.e. purpose of the creation: worship). This is a form of deterioration and we seek Allaah's refuge from it.

This hadith affirms the obligation of patience with the rulers even if they are oppressive and tyrant because you (rulers and their subjects) both will equally stand before Allaah and you (subjects) will be their opponent before Allaah if they oppressed you. Don't ever think that oppression occurring in the Dunya will be tolerated; each will have his/her right back in the Day of Judgment. You will stand with them (rulers) before Allaah and He will judge justly between you. So be patient and await for relief that will inherit yourself tranquility and firmness, and, actually, awaiting for relief is an act of worship; you worship Allaah with this.

---

[58] Recorded by al-Bukhari, book of al-Maghazy, chapter (12) Hadith number (4015), and Muslim, book of Zuhd, chapter: Dunya is the prison of the believer and the paradise of the disbeliever (2961).

HADITH NUMBER 92

And bear in mind that when you await for relief from Allaah, the prophet ﷺ (salallahu 'alayhi wa sallam) promised,

$$\text{وَاعْلَمْ أَنَّ النَّصْرَ مَعَ الصَّبْرِ، وَأَنَّ الْفَرَجَ مَعَ الْكَرَبِ، وَأَنَّ مَعَ الْعُسْرِ يُسْرًا}$$

"And know that victory comes with patience, relief with affliction, and hardship with ease."[59]

This warning of the increasing evil over time and that time will get worse. The prophet ﷺ (salallahu 'alayhi wa sallam) once told his companions,

$$\text{مَنْ يَعِشْ مِنْكُمْ فَسَيَرَى اخْتِلَافًا كَثِيرًا}$$

"Indeed, whomever among you lives longer, he will see much difference."[60]

And I think that—although our life in this world is short compared to those who proceeded us—we are seeing a great deal of differing. We have seen a great deal of differing between the years of old and the present time. A trusted person

---

[59] Recorded by Ahmad in al-Musnad (1/307).
[60] Recorded by Abu Dawud, book of Sunnah, chapter: adhering to the Sunnah (4607), al-Tirmidhi, book of knowledge, chapter: hadiths instructing adherence to the Sunnah and avoidance of innovation (2676), ibn Majah in al-Muqadimmah, chapter: following the path of the rightly guided caliphs (42), and Ahmad in al-Musnad (4/126-127). Al-Tirmidhi classified it as Hasan Sahih (sound and authentic).

informed me that Adhaan of al-Fajr prayer was not to be called in this Masjid (al-Masjid al-Jami') but the front line is full. The people would come to the Masjid to pray Tahajjud; but where are those who pray Tahajjud today? They are very few. Conditions have changed; you would find the person in the past (matches) he prophet's ﷺ statement,

"If you were to rely upon Allaah with the reliance He is due, you would be given provision like the birds: They go out hungry in the morning and come back with full bellies in the evening."[61]

When he gets up in the morning, he would say: O Allaah provide me with sustenance! His heart is closely connected to Allaah (glory be to Him) and thus Allaah grants him what he asked for as for now, most of the people are not mindful that they rely on other than Allaah and whoever do so, he/she is left to it.

It's true that Allaah lately has bestowed His bounties upon the youth without a doubt and I ask Allaah to increase them from His generosity. Allah has bestowed His bounties upon them and they become more mindful of Allaah. You would notice a difference between the (condition) of the

---

[61] Recorded by al-Tirmidhi, book of Zuhd, chapter: Reliance on Allaah (2344); ibn Majah, book of Zuhd, chapter: reliance and certainty (4164), and Ahmad in al-Musnad (1/30-52).

HADITH NUMBER 92

youth lately and their peers in about twenty years ago. You would almost find no one of them in the Masjid back then. As for now, most of the people in the Masjid are from the youth. This a great favor –praise be to Allaah- that we wish to last. Be sure that if the public become righteous, their rulers will be forced to be righteous in return, whatever the case may be.

We hope for our brothers in other countries, for whom Allaah has bestowed righteousness and straightness on the truth, to grant their rulers righteousness. We advise them: Be patient and your rulers will be righteous despite their disapproval as if the subjects are righteous, rulers will be righteous by necessity. We beseech Allaah to grant Muslims' rulers and public righteousness. Certainly, He is the most generous.

EXPLANATION OF RIYAADH SALIHEEN: THE CHAPTER ON HASTENING TO GOOD DEEDS

HADITH NUMBER 93

٩٣- عَنْ أَبِي هُرَيْرَةَ -رَضِيَ اللهُ عَنْهُ- أَنَّ رَسُولَ اللهِ صَلَّى اللهُ عَلَيْهِ وَ سَلَّمَ قَالَ : بَادِرُوا بِالْأَعْمَالِ سَبْعًا ، هَلْ تَنْتَظِرُونَ إِلَّا فَقْرًا مُنْسِيًا ، أَوْ غِنًى مُطْغِيًا ، أَوْ مَرَضًا مُفْسِدًا ، أَوْ هَرَمًا مُفْنِدًا ، أَوْ مَوْتًا مُجْهِزًا ، أَوِ الدَّجَالَ فَشَرٌّ غَائِبٍ يُنْتَظَرُ ، أَوِ السَّاعَةَ فَالسَّاعَةُ أَدْهَى وَ أَمَرُّ . رَوَاهُ التِّرْمَذِي وَ قَالَ : حَدِيثٌ حَسَنٌ .

93- Abu Hurayrah reported that the Messenger of Allaah ﷺ (salallahu alayhi wa sallam) said, **"Hasten to do good deeds before you are overtaken by one of the seven afflictions."** Then (giving a warning) he said, **"Are you waiting for poverty which will make you unmindful of devotion, or prosperity which will make you corrupt, or a disease which will disable you, or senility which will make you mentally unstable, or sudden death which will take you all of a sudden, or Ad-Dajjal (false Messiah) who is the worst expected, or the Hour; and the Hour will be most grievous** and most bitter." [At-Tirmidhi and he graded it: Hadith Hasan][62]

The Explanation

It's formerly mentioned in the previous hadiths that the prophet (salallahu 'alayhi wa sallam) has emphasized on the issue of hastening to do good deeds. The prophet (salallahu 'alayhi wa sallam), in this hadith, referred to various matters where the individual should hasten to do good deeds in order to avoid them.

He stated,

بَادِرُوا بِالْأَعْمَالِ سَبْعًا

"Hasten to do good deeds before you are overtaken by one of the seven afflictions."

This means that there are seven imminent matters encompassing the individual about to befall upon him/her; poverty is one of them

هَلْ تَنْتَظِرُونَ إِلَّا فَقْرًا مُنْسِيًا أَوْ غِنًى مُطْغِيًا

"poverty which will make you unmindful of devotion, or prosperity which will make you corrupt."

---

[62] Recorded by al-Tirmidhi, book of Zuhd, chapter: Hadiths reported about hastening to do good deeds (2309). He said: Hasan Gharīb.

EXPLANATION OF RIYAADH SALIHEEN: THE CHAPTER ON HASTENING TO GOOD DEEDS

The individual leads two kinds of life in terms of sustenance; sometimes Allaah bestows wealth upon him/her and provides him/her with money, children, clan, palace, ships, prestige, and other types of wealth. When the individual perceives himself/herself in such condition, he/she transgresses, becomes arrogant, and refuse to worship Allaah–we seek Allaah's refuge. Allaah says,

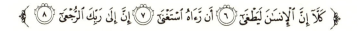

"Nay! Verily, man does transgress (in disbelief and evil deed). Because he considers himself self-sufficient. Surely! unto your Lord is the return." [63]

The verse means: regardless of the degree you (the individual) have reached of self-sufficiency and haughtiness, your return is definitely to Allaah. We ourselves witness that wealth gives rise to corruption –we seek Allaah's refuge. You notice the humility, constant repentance, self-break of the poor individual to Allaah, but if He were to sustain him/her with wealth, he/she would become arrogant and transgressor- we seek refuge in Allaah. On the contrary,

---

[63] Al-'Alaq [96: 6-8]

HADITH NUMBER 93

"poverty that creates unmindful of Allaah's devotion."

Poverty is: insufficiency (i.e. lack of life means) to the extent that the person does not have money. Poverty causes the person to forget plenty of beneficial matters because the person occupies himself/herself with seeking sustenance over other significant matters; this is manifest. Therefore, it's afraid from (potential harm) caused by these two conditions being inflicted on the individual; either overwhelming wealth or poverty that causes unmindfulness.

However, if Allaah bestowed upon the individual an underwhelming wealth and poverty that doesn't cause unmindfulness while leading a normal course of life, constant devotion, and upright life, this is the true happiness of the Dunya.

The true happiness of Dunya is not achieved by wealth because it may lead to transgression; consider Allaah's statement,

﴿ مَنْ عَمِلَ صَالِحًا مِّن ذَكَرٍ أَوْ أُنثَىٰ وَهُوَ مُؤْمِنٌ فَلَنُحْيِيَنَّهُ حَيَاةً طَيِّبَةً وَلَنَجْزِيَنَّهُمْ أَجْرَهُم بِأَحْسَنِ مَا كَانُوا يَعْمَلُونَ ۝ ﴾

"Whoever works righteousness, whether male or female, while he (or she) is a true believer (of Islâmic Monotheism) verily, to him We will give a good life (in this

world with respect, contentment and lawful provision), and We shall pay them certainly a reward in proportion to the best of what they used to do (i.e. Paradise in the Hereafter)." [64]

Allaah didn't say: whoever works with righteousness, whether male or female, We would increase his/her wealth; rather He said,

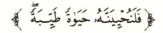

"to him/her We will give a good life."

This good life includes either increase or decrease of wealth. It's reported from the authority of the prophet (salallahu 'alayhi wa sallam) in the Qudsi hadith,

إِنَّ مِنْ عِبَادِي مَنْ لَوْ أَغْنَيْتُهُ لَأَفْسَدَهُ الْغِنَى، وَ
إِنَّ مِنْ عِبَادِي مَنْ لَوْ أَفْقَرْتُهُ لَأَفْسَدَهُ الْفَقْرُ

"Some of My servants would be corrupted by wealth if I were to confer it upon him/her, and some of My servants would be corrupted by poverty if I were to afflict him/her with it."[65]

The third, He said:

---

[64] Al-Nahl [16:97]
[65] - Recorded by Abu Nu'aim in al-Hilyah (8/318-319).

HADITH NUMBER 93

أَوْ مَرَضًا مُفْسِدًا

"a disease which will disable you."

Sickness spoil one's life. In contrast, if the person is healthy, he/she is delighted, tolerant, and intimate; but if sickness befalls, he/she turns to be distressed, intolerant, and selfish. Sickness spoil many things in the human's life; he/she doesn't like company nor expresses cheerfulness with his/her family because he/she is sick and worn out. The human isn't always healthy as sickness might strikes any minute; people may be healthy and active in the morning while sick and week in the evening or vice-versa. Hence, the individual must hasten to do good deeds in fear of being afflicted with such things.

The fourth:

أَوْ هَرَمًا مُفْنِدًا

"senility which will make you mentally unstable"

When the individual gets older and his/her life is extended, he/she has reached to the miserable age as Allaah said,

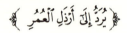

EXPLANATION OF RIYAADH SALIHEEN: THE CHAPTER ON HASTENING TO GOOD DEEDS

"to the miserable old age" [66]

Meaning: the worst age. You find the man whom you know he is among the most wise men and later become like a child or even worse because the child hasn't built up the sense of intellect yet but that man already entertaining the sense of rationality but he has reached to the worst age which is very tough on him. For this reason, we find those who have reached this age harm their family more than children do. The prophet (salallahu 'alayhi wa sallam) sought refuge from reaching to the worst or miserable age.[67]

We ask Allaah's refuge from bringing us to the miserable age because when the person reaches this age, he/she causes inconvenience to himself/herself and to whoever surrounds him/her till the closest person to him/her would wishes death for him/her due to the harm and annoyance he/she creates. This wish may be noticed either by one's speech or actions.

The fifth:

---

[66] An-Nahl [16:70] and Al-Hajj [22:5]
[67] Recorded by al-Bukhari, book of Jihad, chapter: seeking refuge from cowardliness (2822); and
 Muslim, book of remembrance and supplication, chapter: seeking refuge from inability and laziness (2706).

HADITH NUMBER 93

"sudden death which will take you all of a sudden"

Sudden death comes without a warning; the individual may die on his/her bed while sleeping, die on the chair working, or die walking. When the person dies, his/her actions have been ceased as the prophet ﷺ ('alayhi salātu wa sallam) said,

إِذَا مَاتَ ابْنُ آدَمَ انْقَطَعَ عَمَلُهُ إِلَّا مِنْ ثَلَاثَةٍ : إِلَّا مِنْ صَدَقَةٍ جَارِيَةٍ، أَوْ عِلْمٍ يُنْتَفَعُ بِهِ، أَوْ وَلَدٍ صَالِحٍ يَدْعُو لَهُ

"When a man dies, his acts come to an end, but three, recurring charity, or knowledge (by which people) benefit, or a pious son, who prays for him (for the deceased)."[68]

So, hasten to do good deeds before death strikes suddenly which gives you no respite.

The sixth:

أَوِ الدَّجَّالَ فَشَرُّ غَائِبٍ يُنْتَظَرُ

"Ad-Dajjal who is the worst expected."

---

[68] Recorded by Muslim, book of Will, chapter: the reward conferred on the individual after his/her death (1631).

EXPLANATION OF RIYAADH SALIHEEN: THE CHAPTER ON HASTENING TO GOOD DEEDS

Ad-Dajjal is an exaggeration form of ad-Dajjal which is lying and camouflage. (ad-Dajjal) is a man sent by Allaah –Subhaanahu wa Ta'ala- in the end of time. He claims Lordship. This test remains for forty days; a day equal (in length) to a year, a day like a month, a day like a week, and the rest of the days are equal (in length) to the normal days. Allaah –Glory be to Him- supplies him with powers never been given to anybody; He will command the sky, thus it will rain, He will command the earth, thus it will produce vegetation, He will command the earth, thus it will become infertile, and he will command the sky, thus drought will occur and the rain will be prevented. Furthermore, he has a paradise and hell-fire, but they are trickery; his paradise is actually hell-fire while his hell-fire is paradise.

This man is one-eyed and his eye is like a swollen grape. The word **"Kafir"** is written between his two eyes and every believer, whether literate or illiterate would be able to read it.[69] However, both the hypocrite and the disbeliever, even if they are literate, won't be able to read it; this is from Allaah's signs.

Jesus, son of Mary, (alayhi as-sallam) will be sent descending from heavens to kill that man

---

[69] Recorded by al-Bukhari, book of al-Fitan, chapter: Al-Dajjal (7131); and Muslim, book of al-Fitan, chapter: Ad-Dajjal, his description, and his possessions (2933).

HADITH NUMBER 93

(ad-Dajjal) in the gate of Ludd[70] as narrated in some of the hadiths.[71]

The conclusion: ad-Dajjal is an expected evil in the future because his test is very dangerous. Therefore, we supplicate in each prayer: I seek refuge in Allaah from the punishment of the Hell-fire, the punishment of the grave, the test of life and death, and from the test of false Messiah. He was specified because it's considered the most dangerous test in the life of humanity.

The seventh: (or the Hour) Meaning the establishment of the Final Hour where death befalls upon the entire humanity and the Hour will be most grievous and most bitter as Allaah – gory be to Him- said,

﴿ بَلِ ٱلسَّاعَةُ مَوْعِدُهُمْ وَٱلسَّاعَةُ أَدْهَىٰ وَأَمَرُّ ﴾

"Nay, but the Hour is their appointed time (for their full recompense), and the Hour will be more grievous and more bitter." [72]

These are seven matters warned against by the prophet ﷺ (salallahu 'alayhi wa sallam) and ordered us to hasten to do good deeds before (the occurrence) of these matters. Thus,

---

[70] A town close to Jerusalem.
[71] Recorded by Muslim, book of Fitan, chapter: hadiths about ad-Dajjal (2937).
[72] Al-Qamar [54:46]

hasten O Muslim brother/sister before it's too late. You are now vigorous and entertain strength and ability, but there will be a time when you won't be able to do good deeds. Hasten and make yourself accustomed to good deeds and it will adapt and good deeds will be easier to perform. On the contrary, if you make yourself accustomed to laziness and carelessness, it will be disable to do good deeds. We ask Allaah to aid me and you in remembering Him, expressing our gratitude to Him, and worshipping in the best manner.

HADITH NUMBER 94

٩٤- عَنْهُ أَنَّ رَسُولَ الله صَلَّى اللهُ عَلَيْهِ وَ سَلَّمَ قَالَ يَوْمَ خَيْبَرَ : ((لَأُعْطِيَنَّ هَذِهِ الرَّايَةَ رَجُلاً يُحِبُّ اللهَ وَ رَسُولَهُ، يَفْتَحُ اللهُ عَلَى يَدَيْهِ)) قَالَ عُمَرُ رَضِيَ اللهُ عَنْهُ : مَا أَحْبَبْتُ الْإِمَارَةَ إِلَّا يَوْمَئِذٍ، فَتَسَاوَرْتُ لَهَا رَجَاءَ أَنْ أُدْعَى لَهَا، فَدَعَا رَسُولُ الله صَلَّى اللهُ عَلَيْهِ وَ سَلَّمَ عَلِيَّ بْنَ أَبِي طَالِبٍ - رَضِيَ اللهُ عَنْهُ ، فَأَعْطَاهُ إِيَّاهَا، وَ قَالَ : ((امْشِ وَ لَا تَلْتَفِتْ حَتَّى يَفْتَحَ اللهُ عَلَيْكَ)) فَسَارَ عَلِيٌّ شَيْئًا، ثُمَّ وَقَفَ وَ لَمْ يَلْتَفِتْ، فَصَرَخَ : يَا رَسُولَ الله، عَلَى مَاذَا أُقَاتِلُ النَّاسَ ؟ قَالَ : ((قَاتِلْهُمْ حَتَّى يَشْهَدُوا أَنْ لَا إِلَهَ إِلَّا اللهُ ، وَ أَنَّ مُحَمَّدًا رَسُولُ الله ، فَإِذَا فَعَلُوا ذَلِكَ فَقَدْ مَنَعُوا مِنْكَ دِمَاءَهُمْ وَ أَمْوَالَهُمْ إِلَّا بِحَقِّهَا وَ حِسَابُهُمْ عَلَى الله)) . رَوَاهُ مُسْلِمٌ

EXPLANATION OF RIYAADH SALIHEEN: THE CHAPTER ON HASTENING TO GOOD DEEDS

94- On the authority of Abu Hurairah that Allaah's Messenger (salallahu 'alayhi wa sallam) said on the Day of Khaibar:

I shall certainly give this flag in the hand of a man who loves Allaah and his Messenger and Allaah will grant victory at his hand. Umar b. Khattab said: Never did I cherish for leadership but on that day. I came before him with the hope that I may be called for this, but Allaah's Messenger (salallahu 'alayhi wa sallam) called 'Ali b. Abu Talib and he conferred (this honor) upon him and said: Proceed on and do not look about until Allaah grants you victory, and 'Ali went a bit and then halted and did not look about and then said in a loud voice: Allah's Messenger, on what issue should I fight with the people? Thereupon he (the Prophet) said: Fight with them until they bear testimony to the fact that there is no god but Allaah and Muhammad is his Messenger, and when they do that. Then their blood and their riches are inviolable from your hands except that justified by law. and their reckoning is with Allaah." Related by Muslim.[73]

---

[73] Recorded by Muslim, book of: the virtues of the companions, chapter: virtues of Ali ibn Abi Talib –radiallahu 'anhu- (2405).

HADITH NUMBER 94

The Explanation

The author –rahimahullah- related on the authority of Abu Hurairah –radiallahu 'anhu- that the prophet (salallahu 'alayhi wa sallam) said in the day of Khaibar,

لَأُعْطِيَنَّ هَذِهِ الرَّايَةَ رَجُلاً يُحِبُّ اللهَ وَ رَسُولَهُ

"I shall certainly give this flag in the hand of a man who loves Allah and his Messenger."

Day of Khaibar refers to the battle of Khaibar. Khaibar itself were fortresses and farms belong to the Jews; it's located in the northwestward hundred miles away from al-Madinah. The prophet (salallahu 'alayhi wa sallam) conquered it as mentioned in books of his biography.

The Jews were the workers in Khaibar who settled an agreement with the prophet (salallahu 'alayhi wa sallam), after the conquest, that they remain in Khaibar as farmers and shared the half of the harvest while the other half was for Muslims. This settlement remained until they were dislodged to al-Sham and 'Adhru'at by Umar ibn al-Khattab during caliphate. The prophet (salallahu 'alayhi wa sallam) said,

لَأُعْطِيَنَّ هَذِهِ الرَّايَةَ رَجُلاً يُحِبُّ اللهَ وَ رَسُولَهُ

EXPLANATION OF RIYAADH SALIHEEN: THE CHAPTER ON HASTENING TO GOOD DEEDS

"I shall certainly give this flag in the hand of a man who loves Allaah and his Messenger."

The flag is carried by the leader in order for the troops to follow him. **"A man"** the indefinite article signifies unknown person. Umar ibn al-Khattab said:

"Never did I cherish for leadership but on that day."

He wished to be the man whom the prophet (salallahu 'alayhi wa sallam) described.

Therefore, he was looking forward to it and the people spent that night discussing it; each one of them wishes to be the chosen one. In the morning, the prophet (salallahu 'alayhi wa sallam) asked: where is Ali ibn Abi Talib (i.e. his cousin)? They said: O messenger of Allaah! His eyes hurt him. The prophet called him and after he came, the prophet (salallahu 'alayhi wa sallam) spitted on his eyes. Thereupon, his eyes were healed as if he they never hurt him and Allaah has power over everything. The prophet handed him the flag and told him,

امْشِ وَ لَا تَلْتَفِتْ حَتَّى يَفْتَحَ اللهُ

"Proceed on and do not look about until Allaah grants you victory."

HADITH NUMBER 94

He complied with the prophet's command, but he stopped after a while without looking about applying the prophet's command. He shouted in a very loud voice:

O messenger of Allaah! On what issue should I fight with them.

The prophet responded, **"Fight them until they testify that there is no God but Allaah and that Muhammad is His messenger."** This is a very honorable word and if it were to be measured against the earth and heavens, it would become preponderant. The individual leaves disbelief and enters Islam through this testimony; it's the entry of Islam.

فَإِذَا فَعَلُوا ذَلِكَ فَقَدْ مَنَعُوا مِنْكَ دِمَاءَهُمْ وَ أَمْوَالَهُمْ إِلَّا بِحَقِّهَا وَ حِسَابُهُمْ عَلَى الله

"And when they do that then their blood and their riches are inviolable from your hands except that justified by law, and their reckoning is with Allaah."

This (result) is achieved after pronouncing the testimony that there is no God (worthy of worship) but Allah and that Muhammad is His messenger. Subsequently, they are not to be fought and their blood and wealth are inviolable except that justified by Law (i.e. if a violation is committed after the pronunciation of this testimony). This testimony has requirements; it's not just a word to be pronounced by the tongue. It's rather has conditions and requirements that must be observed.

For this reason, when some of the Salaf (early pious scholars) were asked about the prophet's statement, **"The key to paradise is: There is no God (worthy of worship) but Allaah and that Muhammad is His messenger."** He responded: yes, but each key requires teeth (to work properly). He said the truth- rahimahullah. The key requires teeth otherwise it won't work.

His statement **"except that justified by law."** covers whatever nullifies one's belief while still pronouncing the testimony of La ilâh illa Allaah. Whoever disbelieved even if he/she still pronounces La ilâh illa Allaah and committed a nullifier; this testimony won't benefit him/her.

The hypocrites were remembering Allaah by saying: La ilâh illa Allaah and when you look at them, their persons please you; their appearance resembles that of the most perfect believers. They had always said: we, indeed, testify that you are the messenger of Allaah whenever they are with the prophet (salallahu 'alayhi wa sallam). Their testimony includes some intensifiers; the verb (testify), and the word (indeed). Allaah –glory be to Him- responded (o their claim) who knows what hearts conceal,

HADITH NUMBER 94

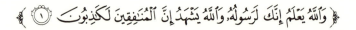

"Allaah knows that you are indeed His Messenger and Allaah bears witness that the hypocrites are liars indeed." [74]

Allaah's witness is against the hypocrites' witness. He bears witness that they are liars indeed. Allaah emphasized their false testimony by three intensifiers. Hence, the blood and wealth are not inviolable for everyone who bears witness that there is no God (worthy of worship) but Allaah because the prophet (salallahu 'alayhi wa sallam) used exclusion form in his saying,

"except that justified by law."

For instance: when some Arabs ceased to give out Zakah after the prophet's death (salallahu 'alayhi wa sallam) and Abu Bakr prepared to fight them, some companions discussed (this decision) with him: how do you fight them and they bear witness that there is no God (worthy of worship) but Allaah? He –radiallahu 'anhu- responded: By Allaah, I will fight whoever separates between prayer and Zakah; Zakah is the right of the wealth (to be given out) and the prophet (sallahu 'alayhi wa sallam) said,

---

[74] Al-Munafiqoon [63:1]

EXPLANATION OF RIYAADH SALIHEEN: THE CHAPTER ON HASTENING TO GOOD DEEDS

إِلَّا بِحَقِّهَا

"except what is justified by law."

He fought them –radiallahu 'anhu- and won the battle- all praise is due to Allaah.

The conclusion: The blood and wealth are not to be inviolable for anyone who pronounces La ilâh illa Allaah; there must be exceptions. Thus, the scholars –rahimahumallah- said," if a town were to leave performing Adhaan (call to prayer) and Iqamah (summon those who pray), they would not be disbelievers, but they are to be fought and their blood will be violable until they observe the Adhaan and Iqamah which are not from the pillars of Islam; they are from the requirements of Islam.

It's said, "if some people haven't observed Eid prayer, which is not from the five obligations, they are to be fought with sword and bullets until they observe praying it. Although Eid prayer is a collective duty, Sunnah as some scholars maintain, or an individual duty based on the preponderant opinion, the point is about the permissibility of fighting Muslims in order that they observe the outward Islamic rituals; this is why he said

"except by what is justified by law."

HADITH NUMBER 94

This hadith proves the permissibility of the individual's statement, "I will do so and so in the future" even if he/she hasn't linked it to "If Allaah wills". We should know the difference between what the person expresses of what is inside himself/herself and what the person intends to do. The former is tolerable even if the person hasn't linked it to, "if Allaah wills because he/she is expressing what is inside himself/herself. As for the latter, if the person intends to do something, he/she must associate it with "if Allaah wills". Allaah says,

"And never say of anything, "I shall do such and such thing tomorrow. Except (with the saying), "If Allaah will!" [75]

There is a difference between the person's expression of what is inside and the person's intention that he/she will do something tomorrow. You don't expect you'll live till tomorrow; you may die before you reach tomorrow or you may not, but still there are some impediments and preventions. In addition, you may stay alive but Allaah diverts your intention away from the thing you intend to do and reality is the proof. It happens frequently that a person may intend to do something in the

---

[75] Al-Kahf [18:23-24]

next day but Allaah drivers him/her away from doing it.

It was said to one of the Arab Bedouins – they, Subhanallah, answer naturally sometimes- "How do you observe your Lord's existence?" He replied, "Footprints signifies walking, the camel's dung signifies camel. So, a sky with constellations, a land with spacious roads, and seas with waves don't signify (the existence) of the All-Hearer the All-Seer. He is an ignorant Bedouin, but he employed his intellect to discover Allah's existence; all of these grandiose objects must be a proof for its Creator and Disposer.

Another one was asked,

"How do you observe the existence of your Lord?" He replied, **"by holding back the determination people may have and diversion of intention by Allaah."**

The individual may determine to do something, then he is held back without perceiving any apparent reason; so who held it back? The one who held back is the same one who created it, namely, Allaah. Likewise, diversion of intentions where the individual intends to do something or even starts doing it, but somehow he is diverted.

We conclude: This hadith proves the permissibility of saying: I will do so and so; if it

HADITH NUMBER 94

he/she just expresses what is inside himself/herself by contrast to expressing a decisive intention of what he/she will do because it's Allaah only who knows the future. There is no harm in expressing what is inside oneself and Allaah is the one that grants success.

NOTES

NOTES

Made in the USA
Middletown, DE
08 November 2024

63682679R00061